HAMLET

William Shakespeare
HAMLET

Edited by
CYRUS HOY

W · W · NORTON & COMPANY · *New York* · *London*

First published as a Norton paperback original 1996

Printed in the United States of America.

The text of this book is composed in Electra, with
the display set in Bernhard Modern. Composition and
manufacturing by The Maple-Vail Book Group.
Book design by Antonina Krass.

ISBN 0-393-31642-4

W.W. Norton & Company, Inc., 500 Fifth Avenue, New York, N.Y. 10110
W. W. Norton & Company, Ltd., 10 Coptic Street, London WC1A 1PU

1 2 3 4 5 6 7 8 9 0

Contents

Preface

Everything about *The Tragedy of Hamlet, Prince of Denmark* is problematic. Critical uncertainty concerning the character of the Prince, his attitudes, and the tragic quality of his highly dramatic situation is matched by a corresponding diversity of scholarly opinion regarding such matters as the date of the play, its precise relation to its sources, and its textual authority. An editor approaches his task with a proper awe that is the more profound from his steady realization that he is, after all, dealing with the most celebrated work in English literature.

The present edition includes a text of the play in modern spelling, with explanatory and textual notes. The text of the present edition of *Hamlet* is based on that of the second quarto, published in 1604-5. Since there is good reason to suppose that the second quarto was printed from Shakespeare's own manuscript, its authority is very high, and I have adhered to it closely, but not slavishly. The second quarto of *Hamlet* is, unfortunately, a very carelessly printed book. It exhibits a number of obvious misreadings, and it is riddled with omissions of all sorts, from single letters to whole lines. In such cases, an editor must turn to other textual authority, usually to the text of the play printed in the 1623 folio collection of Shakespeare's complete works. The folio must be consulted as well for some 80 lines, scattered throughout the play, which are omitted from the second quarto. My editorial practices will be evident from the textual notes, printed after the play, where a complete list of all substantive departures from the text of the second quarto is given. The editorial problem that the play poses is summarized, together with an account of the principles which have governed the preparation of the present edition, in the Textual Commentary section.

The play has never ceased to elicit and sustain critical attention, which is surely one measure of its greatness. A lesser work would have been exhausted long ago. For the early eighteenth century, the play posed no problem. The severest stricture that Dennis, writing in 1712, could level at it was its failure—which it shared with all Shakespeare's tragedies—to observe the law of poetic justice. For the anonymous

author of *Some Remarks on the Tragedy of Hamlet* (1736), the famous
question of why the Prince delayed in avenging his father's murder,
the answer was simple; if he had not delayed, there would have been
no play. For the critics of the Romantic period, the play distinctly
posed a problem; they isolated it in Hamlet's delay to action; and they
found the explanation for his delay in the particular make-up of his
nature. On these issues, critical discussion of the play has turned ever
since, though the best recent criticism has stressed the need to look
beyond the character of the Prince and to view the play in its totality.

Modern criticism of Shakespeare's plays has also drawn attention
to the need to see them in the context of the moral and intellectual
assumptions and attitudes that were current when they were composed. The writings of such figures as Lavater, Primaudaye, and
Montaigne suggest something at least of the climate of late-
Renaissance opinion as this would appear to have affected the conception of Shakespeare's treatment of the Hamlet story. The subjects
of melancholy, demonology, the nature of man, and death, on which
these authors wrote, were, in their several ways, of absorbing interest
to the late Renaissance, and each, in varying degrees, impinges on
important issues raised by *The Tragedy of Hamlet*. The statements of
Shakespeare's contemporaries on these matters warrant the attention
of any serious student of the play. While it may be doubted whether
or not knowledge of late sixteenth-century attitudes toward ghosts, or
the physiological theory of the four humors, will provide the key to the
play's profoundest meanings, there is no doubt at all that the failure to
understand the opinions of Shakespeare's age concerning such matters as these (and one might include the subject of revenge as well)
can seriously impede the effort to deal with the play on its own terms.
The unquiet spirit that haunts the play is, after all, the agent that sets
the action in motion; and Hamlet's melancholy is both the cause and
the effect of a pervasive sense of evil that is the very ambiance of the
tragedy.

Questions concerning the nature of man, and the nature of death,
carry us to the heart of the play. About the nature of man, the
Renaissance was of two minds. The divergent views are recorded,
among other places, in Primaudaye's *French Academy* and
Montaigne's *Apology Of Raymond Sebond*. They have come together,
in Shakespeare, in such a passage as Hamlet's speech beginning
"What a piece of work is a man" (II.ii.288ff.). Whether Shakespeare
had read Montaigne when he wrote *Hamlet* has been much debated
(Florio's translation appeared in the same year — 1603 — as the first edition of the play, but Shakespeare could have seen it in manuscript).
The parallels of thought and language between *Hamlet* and Florio's
rendition of the *Essais* are very striking, but positive proof of a direct

influence at this point in Shakespeare's career is lacking. It does not finally matter. The identity of feeling and thought evident again and again in the essays and the tragedy is the important thing, however one accounts for it. The great passage on death, time, and change, at the end of the *Apology of Raymond Sebond*, might be spoken at any number of points in *Hamlet*. In effect, it is. "And nothing remaineth or ever continueth in one state," says Montaigne. "And nothing is at a like goodness still," says Claudius at one of the most impressive moments in the play (IV.vii. 114). "If we should ever continue one and the same, how is it then that now we rejoice at one thing, and now at another?" asks Montaigne. "How comes it to pass we love things contrary, or we hate them * * *?" This is as much as to ask what Hamlet is agonizingly asking himself from the beginning of the play: how his mother could so readily transfer her affections from her Hyperionlike first husband to his satyrlike brother—a question that he puts to her directly in the course of the scene in her chamber ("Could you on this fair mountain leave to feed, / And batten on this moor?" [III.iv.67-68]). This is but a single demonstration, in a play that abounds with like examples, of the contradictory nature of reality, as Montaigne defines it. He does so in terms of its most profound metaphysical implications—implications that take the form of a series of bewildering paradoxes.

How is it that we have different affections, holding no more the same sense in the same thought? For it is not likely that without alteration we should take other passions, and *what admitteth alterations, continueth not the same*; and if it be not one selfsame, then is it not; but rather with being all one, the simple being doth also change, ever becoming other from other. And by consequence, nature's senses are deceived and lie falsely; taking what appeareth for what is; for want of truly knowing what it is that is.

The paradoxes are present in *Hamlet*, where they have been raised to the power of so many tragic truths: tragic because they point directly to as many appalling contradictions in the nature of things. Appearance contradicts reality, words contradict deeds, behavior contradicts purpose; nothing is what it appears to be, and nothing endures, least of all the high dedication of a passionate moment.

What to ourselves in passion we purpose,
The passion ending, doth the purpose lose.   (III.ii.176-77)

Thus the Player King to the Player Queen, in answer to her loud protestations of eternal fidelity. If, in the context, the words reflect most immediately upon Gertrude, they reflect as well upon her son, who has also proposed something to himself in a fit of passion, just after his first encounter with the ghost. Ironically enough, it is the other King, the one of shreds and patches, who has the final comment on this matter, which involves nothing less than the need, so urgently felt by the tragic protagonist throughout the play, for suiting the action to the word, the word to the action.

> That we would do,
> We should do when we would; for this "would" changes,
> And hath abatements and delays as many
> As there are tongues, are hands, are accidents,
> And then this "should" is like a spendthrift sigh
> That hurts by easing.   (IV.vii.116-21)

Any modern editor of a Shakespearean play is heavily indebted to the work that has been done in the field of textual bibliography over the past half century. My own indebtedness to the work of the late W. W. Greg will be evident to anyone familiar with the problems of Elizabethan textual criticism. I have also laid under heavy contribution studies of the second quarto of *Hamlet* by F. T. Bowers and J. R. Brown, and of the folio text by Charlton Hinman and Harold Jenkins. Professor Jenkins's account of actors' interpolations in the folio text, to which reference is made in the notes and Textual Commentary, has been a source of continual enlightenment to me throughout the preparation of this edition. To him and it, I have a special obligation which I gratefully record. To the staffs of the Folger Shakespeare Library, Washington, D.C., where work on this edition was begun, and the Bodleian Library, Oxford, where it was completed, I wish to acknowledge my appreciation for many courtesies.

CYRUS HOY

October 1962

Preface to the Second Edition

During the more than quarter of a century since this edition was first published, the text of *Hamlet* has continued to be a problem, and it always will be on the evidence that is currently available. Though the debate continues as to whether a modern edition of the play should be based on the second quarto (1604–5) or the first folio (1623), I persist in the belief that, all things considered, the second quarto provides the more authoritative text, and it remains the textual basis for this edition.

In preparing this revised Norton edition, I have been principally concerned with refining the punctuation and stage directions for the play, and expanding the scope of the commentary notes on its language and action.

CYRUS HOY

May 1992

HAMLET

THE
Tragicall Historie of
HAMLET,
Prince of Denmarke.

By William Shakespeare.

Newly imprinted and enlarged to almoſt as much
againe as it was, according to the true and perfect
Coppie.

AT LONDON,
Printed by I. R. for N. L. and are to be ſold at his
ſhoppe vnder Saint Dunſtons Church in
Fleetſtreet. 1 6.0.4.

[Dramatis Personae

CLAUDIUS, *King of Denmark.*
HAMLET, *son to the former and nephew to the present King.*
POLONIUS, *Lord Chamberlain.*
HORATIO, *friend to Hamlet.*
LAERTES, *son to Polonius.*
VOLTEMAND,
CORNELIUS,
ROSENCRANTZ,
GUILDENSTERN, } *courtiers.*
OSRIC,
A GENTLEMAN,
A PRIEST.

MARCELLUS,
BERNARDO, } *officers.*
FRANCISCO, *a soldier.*
REYNALDO, *servant to Polonius.*
PLAYERS.
TWO CLOWNS, *grave-diggers.*
FORTINBRAS, *Prince of Norway.*
A NORWEGIAN CAPTAIN.

ENGLISH AMBASSADORS.
GERTRUDE, *Queen of Denmark, and mother of Hamlet.*
OPHELIA, *daughter to Polonius.*

GHOST OF HAMLET'S FATHER.

LORDS, LADIES, OFFICERS, SOLDIERS, SAILORS, MESSENGERS, *and* ATTENDANTS.

SCENE: *Denmark.*]

Hamlet

[I.i]

Enter BERNARDO *and* FRANCISCO, *two sentinels.*

BER. Who's there?

FRAN. Nay, answer me. Stand and unfold yourself.

BER. Long live the king!

FRAN. Bernardo?

BER. He.   5

FRAN. You come most carefully upon your hour.

BER. 'Tis now struck twelve. Get thee to bed, Francisco.

FRAN. For this relief much thanks. 'Tis bitter cold,
And I am sick at heart.

BER. Have you had quiet guard?

FRAN.   Not a mouse stirring.   10

BER. Well, good night.
If you do meet Horatio and Marcellus,
The rivals of my watch, bid them make haste.

Enter HORATIO *and* MARCELLUS.

FRAN. I think I hear them. Stand, ho! Who is there?

HOR. Friends to this ground.

MAR.   And liegemen to the Dane.   15

FRAN. Give you good night.

MAR.   O, farewell, honest soldier!
Who hath relieved you?

FRAN.   Bernardo hath my place.
Give you good night.   *Exit* FRANCISCO.

MAR.   Holla, Bernardo!

BER.   Say—
What, is Horatio there?

HOR.   A piece of him.

BER. Welcome, Horatio. Welcome, good Marcellus.   20

HOR. What, has this thing appeared again to-night?

BER. I have seen nothing.

MAR. Horatio says 'tis but our fantasy,
And will not let belief take hold of him
Touching this dreaded sight twice seen of us.   25

Therefore I have entreated him along
With us to watch the minutes of this night,
That if again this apparition come,
He may approve our eyes and speak to it.
HOR.   Tush, tush, 'twill not appear.
BER.   Sit down awhile,   30
And let us once again assail your ears,
That are so fortified against our story,
What we have two nights seen.
HOR.   Well, sit we down,
And let us hear Bernardo speak of this.
BER.   Last night of all,   35
When yond same star that's westward from the pole
Had made his course t' illume that part of heaven
Where now it burns, Marcellus and myself,
The bell then beating one—

            Enter GHOST.
MAR.   Peace, break thee off. Look where it comes again.   40
BER.   In the same figure like the king that's dead.
MAR.   Thou art a scholar; speak to it, Horatio.
BER.   Looks 'a not like the king? Mark it, Horatio.
HOR.   Most like. It harrows me with fear and wonder.
BER.   It would be spoke to.
MAR.   Question it, Horatio.   45
HOR.   What art thou that usurp'st this time of night
Together with that fair and warlike form
In which the majesty of buried Denmark
Did sometimes march? By heaven I charge thee, speak.
MAR.   It is offended.
BER.   See, it stalks away.   50
HOR.   Stay. Speak, speak. I charge thee, speak.   *Exit* GHOST.
MAR.   'Tis gone and will not answer.
BER.   How now, Horatio! You tremble and look pale.
Is not this something more than fantasy?
What think you on't?   55
HOR.   Before my God, I might not this believe
Without the sensible and true avouch
Of mine own eyes.
MAR.   Is it not like the king?
HOR.   As thou art to thyself.
Such was the very armor he had on   60
When he the ambitious Norway combated.
So frowned he once when, in an angry parle,

29. *approve* confirm.   49. *sometimes* formerly.
36. *pole* polestar.   57. *sensible* confirmed by one of the senses.
44. *harrows* afflicts, distresses.   61. *Norway* King of Norway.
48. *buried Denmark* the buried King of Denmark.   62. *parle* parley.

He smote the sledded Polacks on the ice.
'Tis strange.
MAR. Thus twice before, and jump at this dead hour,   65
    With martial stalk hath he gone by our watch.
HOR. In what particular thought to work I know not,
    But in the gross and scope of mine opinion,
    This bodes some strange eruption to our state.
MAR. Good now, sit down, and tell me he that knows,   70
    Why this same strict and most observant watch
    So nightly toils the subject of the land,
    And why such daily cast of brazen cannon
    And foreign mart for implements of war;
    Why such impress of shipwrights, whose sore task   75
    Does not divide the Sunday from the week.
    What might be toward that this sweaty haste
    Doth make the night joint-laborer with the day?
    Who is't that can inform me?
HOR.   That can I.
    At least, the whisper goes so. Our last king,   80
    Whose image even but now appeared to us,
    Was as you know by Fortinbras of Norway,
    Thereto pricked on by a most emulate pride,
    Dared to the combat; in which our valiant Hamlet
    (For so this side of our known world esteemed him)   85
    Did slay this Fortinbras; who by a sealed compact
    Well ratified by law and heraldry,
    Did forfeit, with his life, all those his lands
    Which he stood seized of, to the conqueror;
    Against the which a moiety competent   90
    Was gagéd by our king; which had returned
    To the inheritance of Fortinbras,
    Had he been vanquisher; as, by the same comart
    And carriage of the article designed,
    His fell to Hamlet. Now, sir, young Fortinbras,   95
    Of unimprovéd mettle hot and full,
    Hath in the skirts of Norway here and there
    Sharked up a list of lawless resolutes
    For food and diet to some enterprise
    That hath a stomach in't; which is no other,   100

63. *sledded Polacks* the Poles mounted on sleds or
sledges.
65. *jump* just, exactly.
68. *gross and scope* general drift.
72. *toils* causes to toil; *subject* people.
74. *mart* traffic, bargaining.
75. *impress* conscription.
77. *toward* imminent, impending.
83. *emulate* ambitious.
87. *heraldry* the law of arms, regulating tourna-
ments and state combats.
89. *seized* possessed.
90. *moiety competent* sufficient portion.
91. *gaged* pledged.
93. *comart* joint bargain.
94. *carriage* import.
96. *unimproved* unrestrained.
98. *Sharked up* picked up indiscriminately.
100. *stomach* spice of adventure.

As it doth well appear unto our state,
But to recover of us by strong hand
And terms compulsatory, those foresaid lands
So by his father lost; and this, I take it,
Is the main motive of our preparations,   105
The source of this our watch, and the chief head
Of this post-haste and romage in the land.
BER.   I think it be no other but e'en so.
Well may it sort that this portentous figure
Comes arméd through our watch so like the king   110
That was and is the question of these wars.
HOR.   A mote it is to trouble the mind's eye.
In the most high and palmy state of Rome,
A little ere the mightiest Julius fell,
The graves stood tenantless, and the sheeted dead   115
Did squeak and gibber in the Roman streets;
As stars with trains of fire, and dews of blood,
Disasters in the sun; and the moist star,
Upon whose influence Neptune's empire stands,
Was sick almost to doomsday with eclipse.   120
And even the like precurse of feared events,
As harbingers preceding still the fates
And prologue to the omen coming on,
Have heaven and earth together demonstrated
Unto our climatures and countrymen.   125

        Enter GHOST.
But soft, behold, lo where it comes again!
I'll cross it though it blast me.—Stay, illusion.
                        [GHOST] *spreads his arms.*
If thou hast any sound or use of voice,
Speak to me.
If there be any good thing to be done,   130
That may to thee do ease, and grace to me,
Speak to me.
If thou art privy to thy country's fate,
Which happily foreknowing may avoid,
O, speak!   135
Or if thou hast uphoarded in thy life
Extorted treasure in the womb of earth,
For which, they say, you spirits oft walk in death,
                        The cock crows.

106. *head* fountainhead.
107. *romage* turmoil.
109. *sort* suit, be in accordance.
112. *mote* particle of dust.
113. *palmy* flourishing.
115. *sheeted* in shrouds.
118. *Disasters* ominous signs; *moist star* the moon.

121. *precurse* heralding, foreshadowing.
122. *harbingers* forerunners; *still* ever.
123. *omen* ominous event.
125. *climatures* regions.
127. *cross it* cross its path.
134. *happily* haply, perchance.

Speak of it. Stay, and speak. Stop it, Marcellus.

MAR.   Shall I strike at it with my partisan?   140

HOR.   Do, if it will not stand.

BER.   'Tis here.

HOR.   'Tis here.

MAR.   'Tis gone.   [*Exit* GHOST.]

We do it wrong, being so majestical,

To offer it the show of violence;

For it is as the air, invulnerable,   145

And our vain blows malicious mockery.

BER.   It was about to speak when the cock crew.

HOR.   And then it started like a guilty thing

Upon a fearful summons. I have heard

The cock, that is the trumpet to the morn,   150

Doth with his lofty and shrill-sounding throat

Awake the god of day, and at his warning,

Whether in sea or fire, in earth or air,

Th' extravagant and erring spirit hies

To his confine; and of the truth herein   155

This present object made probation.

MAR.   It faded on the crowing of the cock.

Some say that ever 'gainst that season comes

Wherein our Savior's birth is celebrated,

This bird of dawning singeth all night long,   160

And then, they say, no spirit dare stir abroad,

The nights are wholesome, then no planets strike,

No fairy takes, nor witch hath power to charm,

So hallowed and so gracious is that time.

HOR.   So have I heard and do in part believe it.   165

But look, the morn in russet mantle clad

Walks o'er the dew of yon high eastward hill.

Break we our watch up, and by my advice

Let us impart what we have seen to-night

Unto young Hamlet, for upon my life   170

This spirit, dumb to us, will speak to him.

Do you consent we shall acquaint him with it,

As needful in our loves, fitting our duty?

MAR.   Let's do't, I pray, and I this morning know

Where we shall find him most convenient.   *Exeunt.*   175

---

140. *partisan* pike.
154. *extravagant* straying, vagrant; *erring* wandering.
156. *probation* proof.

158. *'gainst* just before.
162. *strike* blast, destroy by malign influence.
163. *takes* bewitches.

[I.ii]

Flourish. Enter CLAUDIUS KING OF DENMARK, GERTRUDE THE
QUEEN, COUNCILLORS [*including*] POLONIUS, *and his son*
LAERTES, HAMLET, *cum aliis* [*including* VOLTEMAND
and CORNELIUS.]

KING. Though yet of Hamlet our dear brother's death
  The memory be green, and that it us befitted
  To bear our hearts in grief, and our whole kingdom
  To be contracted in one brow of woe,
  Yet so far hath discretion fought with nature   5
  That we with wisest sorrow think on him,
  Together with remembrance of ourselves.
  Therefore our sometime sister, now our queen,
  Th' imperial jointress to this warlike state,
  Have we, as 'twere with a defeated joy,   10
  With an auspicious and a dropping eye,
  With mirth in funeral, and with dirge in marriage,
  In equal scale weighing delight and dole,
  Taken to wife; nor have we herein barred
  Your better wisdoms, which have freely gone   15
  With this affair along. For all, our thanks.
  Now follows that you know young Fortinbras,
  Holding a weak supposal of our worth,
  Or thinking by our late dear brother's death
  Our state to be disjoint and out of frame,   20
  Colleaguéd with this dream of his advantage,
  He hath not failed to pester us with message
  Importing the surrender of those lands
  Lost by his father, with all bands of law,
  To our most valiant brother. So much for him.   25
  Now for ourself, and for this time of meeting,
  Thus much the business is: we have here writ
  To Norway, uncle of young Fortinbras—
  Who, impotent and bedrid, scarcely hears
  Of this his nephew's purpose—to suppress   30
  His further gait herein, in that the levies,
  The lists, and full proportions are all made
  Out of his subject; and we here dispatch
  You, good Cornelius, and you, Voltemand,
  For bearers of this greeting to old Norway,   35
  Giving to you no further personal power
  To business with the king, more than the scope
  Of these delated articles allow.

[I.ii] 0.3 *cum aliis* with others
9. *jointress* a window who holds a jointure or life
interest in an estate.
14. *barred* excluded.

21. *Colleagued* united.
31. *gait* proceeding.
32. *proportions* forces or supplies for war.
38. *delated* expressly stated.

Farewell, and let your haste commend your duty.

COR. ⎫
VOL. ⎭ In that, and all things will we show our duty.   40

KING. We doubt it nothing, heartily farewell.

[*Exeunt* VOLTEMAND *and* CORNELIUS.]

And now, Laertes, what's the news with you?
You told us of some suit. What is't, Laertes?
You cannot speak of reason to the Dane
And lose your voice. What wouldst thou beg, Laertes,   45
That shall not be my offer, not thy asking?
The head is not more native to the heart,
The hand more instrumental to the mouth,
Than is the throne of Denmark to thy father.
What wouldst thou have, Laertes?

LAER.   My dread lord,   50
Your leave and favor to return to France,
From whence, though willingly, I came to Denmark
To show my duty in your coronation,
Yet now I must confess, that duty done,
My thoughts and wishes bend again toward France,   55
And bow them to your gracious leave and pardon.

KING. Have you your father's leave? What says Polonius?

POL. He hath, my lord, wrung from me my slow leave
By laborsome petition, and at last
Upon his will I sealed my hard consent.   60
I do beseech you give him leave to go.

KING. Take thy fair hour, Laertes. Time be thine,
And thy best graces spend it at thy will.
But now, my cousin Hamlet, and my son—

HAM. [*Aside.*] A little more than kin, and less than kind.   65

KING. How is it that the clouds still hang on you?

HAM. Not so, my lord. I am too much in the sun.

QUEEN. Good Hamlet, cast thy nighted color off,
And let thine eye look like a friend on Denmark.
Do not for ever with thy vailéd lids   70
Seek for thy noble father in the dust.
Thou know'st 'tis common—all that lives must die,
Passing through nature to eternity.

HAM. Ay, madam, it is common.

QUEEN.   If it be,
Why seems it so particular with thee?   75

HAM. Seems, madam? Nay, it is. I know not 'seems.'

---

44. *Dane* King of Denmark.
45. *lose your voice* speak in vain.
47. *native* joined by nature.
48. *instrumental* serviceable.
56. *pardon* indulgence.
60. *hard* reluctant.

64. *cousin* kinsman of any kind except parent, child, brother or sister.
65. *kin* related as nephew; *kind* (1) affectionate (2) natural, lawful.
70. *vailed* lowered.
75. *particular* personal, individual.

'Tis not alone my inky cloak, good mother,
Nor customary suits of solemn black,
Nor windy suspiration of forced breath,
No, nor the fruitful river in the eye,   80
Nor the dejected haviour of the visage,
Together with all forms, moods, shapes of grief,
That can denote me truly. These indeed seem,
For they are actions that a man might play,
But I have that within which passes show—   85
These but the trappings and the suits of woe.
KING.   'Tis sweet and commendable in your nature, Hamlet,
To give these mourning duties to your father,
But you must know your father lost a father,
That father lost, lost his, and the survivor bound   90
In filial obligation for some term
To do obsequious sorrow. But to persever
In obstinate condolement is a course
Of impious stubbornness. 'Tis unmanly grief.
It shows a will most incorrect to heaven,   95
A heart unfortified, a mind impatient,
An understanding simple and unschooled.
For what we know must be, and is as common
As any the most vulgar thing to sense,
Why should we in our peevish opposition   100
Take it to heart? Fie, 'tis a fault to heaven,
A fault against the dead, a fault to nature,
To reason most absurd, whose common theme
Is death of fathers, and who still hath cried,
From the first corse till he that died to-day,   105
'This must be so.' We pray you throw to earth
This unprevailing woe, and think of us
As of a father, for let the world take note
You are the most immediate to our throne,
And with no less nobility of love   110
Than that which dearest father bears his son
Do I impart toward you. For your intent
In going back to school in Wittenberg,
It is most retrograde to our desire,
And we beseech you, bend you to remain   115
Here in the cheer and comfort of our eye,
Our chiefest courtier, cousin, and our son.
QUEEN.   Let not thy mother lose her prayers, Hamlet.
I pray thee stay with us, go not to Wittenberg.
HAM.   I shall in all my best obey you, madam.   120

---

92. *obsequious* dutiful in performing funeral ob-   105. *corse* corpse.
sequies or manifesting regard for the dead; *persever* 114. *retrograde* contrary.
persevere.

KING. Why, 'tis a loving and a fair reply.
Be as ourself in Denmark. Madam, come.
This gentle and unforced accord of Hamlet
Sits smiling to my heart, in grace whereof,
No jocund health that Denmark drinks to-day   125
But the great cannon to the clouds shall tell,
And the king's rouse the heaven shall bruit again,
Respeaking earthly thunder. Come away.
                              Flourish. Exeunt all but HAMLET.
HAM. O, that this too too sallied flesh would melt,
Thaw, and resolve itself into a dew,   130
Or that the Everlasting had not fixed
His canon 'gainst self-slaughter. O God, God,
How weary, stale, flat, and unprofitable
Seem to me all the uses of this world!
Fie on't, ah, fie, 'tis an unweeded garden   135
That grows to seed. Things rank and gross in nature
Possess it merely. That it should come to this,
But two months dead, nay, not so much, not two.
So excellent a king, that was to this
Hyperion to a satyr, so loving to my mother,   140
That he might not beteem the winds of heaven
Visit her face too roughly. Heaven and earth,
Must I remember? Why, she would hang on him
As if increase of appetite had grown
By what it fed on, and yet, within a month—   145
Let me not think on't. Frailty, thy name is woman—
A little month, or ere those shoes were old
With which she followed my poor father's body
Like Niobe, all tears, why she—
O God, a beast that wants discourse of reason   150
Would have mourned longer—married with my uncle,
My father's brother, but no more like my father
Than I to Hercules. Within a month,
Ere yet the salt of most unrighteous tears
Had left the flushing in her gallèd eyes,   155

---

127. *rouse* full draught of liquor; *bruit* echo.
129. *sallied* sullied. "Sallied" is the reading of Q2
(and Q1). F reads "solid." Since Hamlet's primary
concern is with the fact of the flesh's impurity, not
with its corporeality, the choice as between Q and
F clearly lies with Q. "Sally" is a legitimate sixteenth-century form of "sully"; it occurs in Dek-
ker's *Patient Grissil* (I.i.12), printed in 1603, as F.
T. Bowers has pointed out (in "Hamlet's 'Sullied'
or 'Solid' Flesh. A Bibliographical Case-History,"
Shakespeare Survey 9 [1956]: p. 44); and it occurs
as a noun at II.i.39 of *Hamlet*.
132. *canon* law.

137. *merely* entirely.
140. *Hyperion* the sun god.
141. *beteem* allowed.
149. *Niobe* wife of Amphion, King of Thebes, she
boasted of having more children than Leto and was
punished when her seven sons and seven daughters were slain by Apollo and Artemis, children of
Leto; in her grief she was changed by Zeus into a
stone, which continually dropped tears.
150. *wants* lacks; *discourse of reason* the reasoning
faculty.
155. *galled* sore from rubbing or chafing.

She married. O, most wicked speed, to post
With such dexterity to incestuous sheets!
It is not, nor it cannot come to good.
But break my heart, for I must hold my tongue.

Enter HORATIO, MARCELLUS, *and* BERNARDO.

HOR.   Hail to your lordship!
HAM.   I am glad to see you well.   160
Horatio—or I do forget myself.
HOR.   The same, my lord, and your poor servant ever.
HAM.   Sir, my good friend, I'll change that name with you.
And what make you from Wittenberg, Horatio?
Marcellus?   165
MAR.   My good lord!
HAM.   I am very glad to see you. [*To* BERNARDO.] Good even, sir.—
But what, in faith, make you from Wittenberg?
HOR.   A truant disposition, good my lord.
HAM.   I would not hear your enemy say so,   170
Nor shall you do my ear that violence
To make it truster of your own report
Against yourself. I know you are no truant.
But what is your affair in Elsinore?
We'll teach you to drink deep ere you depart.   175
HOR.   My lord, I came to see your father's funeral.
HAM.   I prithee do not mock me, fellow-student,
I think it was to see my mother's wedding.
HOR.   Indeed, my lord, it followed hard upon.
HAM.   Thrift, thrift, Horatio. The funeral baked meats   180
Did coldly furnish forth the marriage tables.
Would I had met my dearest foe in heaven
Or ever I had seen that day, Horatio!
My father—methinks I see my father.
HOR.   Where, my lord?
HAM.   In my mind's eye, Horatio.   185
HOR.   I saw him once, 'a was a goodly king.
HAM.   'A was a man, take him for all in all,
I shall not look upon his like again.
HOR.   My lord, I think I saw him yesternight.
HAM.   Saw who?   190
HOR.   My lord, the king your father.
HAM.   The king my father?
HOR.   Season your admiration for a while
With an attent ear till I may deliver
Upon the witness of these gentlemen

163. *change* exchange.
164. *make* do.
182. *dearest* direst.

192. *Season* temper, moderate; *admiration* wonder, astonishment.

This marvel to you.

HAM.   For God's love, let me hear!   195

HOR.   Two nights together had these gentlemen,
Marcellus and Bernardo, on their watch
In the dead waste and middle of the night
Been thus encountered. A figure like your father,
Armed at point exactly, cap-a-pe,   200
Appears before them, and with solemn march
Goes slow and stately by them. Thrice he walked
By their oppressed and fear-surprisèd eyes
Within his truncheon's length, whilst they, distilled
Almost to jelly with the act of fear,   205
Stand dumb and speak not to him. This to me
In dreadful secrecy impart they did,
And I with them the third night kept the watch,
Where, as they had delivered, both in time,
Form of the thing, each word made true and good,   210
The apparition comes. I knew your father.
These hands are not more like.

HAM.   But where was this?

MAR.   My lord, upon the platform where we watch.

HAM.   Did you not speak to it?

HOR.   My lord, I did,
But answer made it none. Yet once methought   215
It lifted up it head and did address
Itself to motion, like as it would speak;
But even then the morning cock crew loud,
And at the sound it shrunk in haste away
And vanished from our sight.

HAM.   'Tis very strange.   220

HOR.   As I do live, my honored lord, 'tis true,
And we did think it writ down in our duty
To let you know of it.

HAM.   Indeed, sirs, but
This troubles me. Hold you the watch to-night?

ALL.   We do, my lord.

HAM.   Armed, say you?

ALL.   Armed, my lord.   225

HAM.   From top to toe?

ALL.   My lord, from head to foot.

HAM.   Then saw you not his face.

HOR.   O yes, my lord, he wore his beaver up.

HAM.   What, looked he frowningly?

HOR.   A countenance more in sorrow than in anger.   230

---

200. *at point exactly* in every particular; *cap-a-pe*
from head to foot.
204. *truncheon* military leader's baton.

216. *it* its.
228. *beaver* the part of the helmet that was drawn
down to cover the face.

HAM. Pale or red?
HOR. Nay, very pale.
HAM.   And fixed his eyes upon you?
HOR. Most constantly.
HAM.   I would I had been there.
HOR. It would have much amazed you.
HAM.   Very like.
Stayed it long?
HOR. While one with moderate haste might tell a hundred.   235
BOTH. Longer, longer.
HOR.   Not when I saw't.
HAM. His beard was grizzled, no?
HOR. It was as I have seen it in his life,
A sable silvered.
HAM.   I will watch to-night.
Perchance 'twill walk again.
HOR.   I warr'nt it will.   240
HAM. If it assume my noble father's person,
I'll speak to it though hell itself should gape
And bid me hold my peace. I pray you all,
If you have hitherto concealed this sight,
Let it be tenable in your silence still,   245
And whatsomever else shall hap to-night,
Give it an understanding but no tongue.
I will requite your loves. So fare you well.
Upon the platform 'twixt eleven and twelve
I'll visit you.
ALL.   Our duty to your honor.   250
HAM. Your loves, as mine to you. Farewell.
                              Exeunt [all but HAMLET].
My father's spirit in arms? All is not well.
I doubt some foul play. Would the night were come!
Till then sit still, my soul. Foul deeds will rise,
Though all the earth o'erwhelm them, to men's eyes.   *Exit.* 255

[I.iii]

          Enter LAERTES *and* OPHELIA *his sister.*
LAER. My necessaries are embarked. Farewell.
And, sister, as the winds give benefit
And convoy is assistant, do not sleep,
But let me hear from you.
OPH.   Do you doubt that?

---

235. *tell* count.
237. *grizzled* grayish.
239. *sable silvered* black mixed with white.

245. *tenable* retained.
246. *whatsomever* whatsoever.
253. *doubt* suspect.

LAER.   For Hamlet, and the trifling of his favor,   5
        Hold it a fashion and a toy in blood,
        A violet in the youth of primy nature,
        Forward, not permanent, sweet, not lasting,
        The perfume and suppliance of a minute,
        No more.
OPH.   No more but so?
LAER.   Think it no more.   10
        For nature crescent does not grow alone
        In thews and bulk, but as this temple waxes
        The inward service of the mind and soul
        Grows wide withal. Perhaps he loves you now,
        And now no soil nor cautel doth besmirch   15
        The virtue of his will, but you must fear,
        His greatness weighed, his will is not his own,
        For he himself is subject to his birth.
        He may not, as unvalued persons do,
        Carve for himself, for on his choice depends   20
        The safety and health of this whole state,
        And therefore must his choice be circumscribed
        Unto the voice and yielding of that body
        Whereof he is the head. Then if he says he loves you,
        It fits your wisdom so far to believe it   25
        As he in his particular act and place
        May give his saying deed, which is no further
        Than the main voice of Denmark goes withal.
        Then weigh what loss your honor may sustain
        If with too credent ear you list his songs,   30
        Or lose your heart, or your chaste treasure open
        To his unmastered importunity.
        Fear it, Ophelia, fear it, my dear sister,
        And keep you in the rear of your affection,
        Out of the shot and danger of desire.   35
        The chariest maid is prodigal enough
        If she unmask her beauty to the moon.
        Virtue itself scapes not calumnious strokes.
        The canker galls the infants of the spring
        Too oft before their buttons be disclosed,   40

[I.iii] 6. *fashion* the creation of a season only; *toy in blood* passing fancy.
7. *primy* of the springtime.
11. *crescent* growing.
12. *thews* sinews, strength; *this temple* the body.
15. *cautel* deceit.
16. *will* desire.
17. *greatness weighed* high position considered.
19. *unvalued persons* persons of no social importance.

20. *Carve for himself* act according to his own inclination.
23. *yielding* assent.
30. *credent* trusting.
34. *affection* feeling.
39. *canker* canker-worm (which feeds on roses); *galls* injures.
40. *buttons* buds.

And in the morn and liquid dew of youth
Contagious blastments are most imminent.
Be wary then; best safety lies in fear.
Youth to itself rebels, though none else near.
OPH.   I shall the effect of this good lesson keep   45
As watchman to my heart. But, good my brother,
Do not as some ungracious pastors do,
Show me the steep and thorny way to heaven,
Whiles like a puffed and reckless libertine
Himself the primrose path of dalliance treads   50
And recks not his own rede.
LAER.   O, fear me not.

    Enter POLONIUS.

I stay too long. But here my father comes.
A double blessing is a double grace;
Occasion smiles upon a second leave.
POL.   Yet here, Laertes? Aboard, aboard, for shame!   55
The wind sits in the shoulder of your sail,
And you are stayed for. There, my blessing with thee,
And these few precepts in thy memory
Look thou character. Give thy thoughts no tongue,
Nor any unproportioned thought his act.   60
Be thou familiar, but by no means vulgar.
Those friends thou hast, and their adoption tried,
Grapple them unto thy soul with hoops of steel,
But do not dull thy palm with entertainment
Of each new-hatched, unfledged courage. Beware   65
Of entrance to a quarrel, but being in,
Bear't that th' opposéd may beware of thee.
Give every man thy ear, but few thy voice;
Take each man's censure, but reserve thy judgment.
Costly thy habit as thy purse can buy,   70
But not expressed in fancy; rich not gaudy,
For the apparel oft proclaims the man,
And they in France of the best rank and station
Are of a most select and generous chief in that.
Neither a borrower nor a lender be,   75
For loan oft loses both itself and friend,
And borrowing dulls th' edge of husbandry.
This above all, to thine own self be true,
And it must follow as the night the day

42. *blastments* blights.
51. *recks* regards; *rede* counsel.
59. *character* engrave.
60. *unproportioned* inordinate.

61. *vulgar* common.
65. *courage* young blood, man of spirit.
74. *chief* eminence.
77. *husbandry* thriftiness.

Thou canst not then be false to any man.   80
Farewell. My blessing season this in thee!
LAER.   Most humbly do I take my leave, my lord.
POL.   The time invites you. Go, your servants tend.
LAER.   Farewell, Ophelia, and remember well
What I have said to you.
OPH.   'Tis in my memory locked,   85
And you yourself shall keep the key of it.
LAER.   Farewell.   *Exit* LAERTES.
POL.   What is't, Ophelia, he hath said to you?
OPH.   So please you, something touching the Lord Hamlet.
POL.   Marry, well bethought.   90
'Tis told me he hath very oft of late
Given private time to you, and you yourself
Have of your audience been most free and bounteous.
If it be so—as so 'tis put on me,
And that in way of caution—I must tell you,   95
You do not understand yourself so clearly
As it behooves my daughter and your honor.
What is between you? Give me up the truth.
OPH.   He hath, my lord, of late made many tenders
Of his affection to me.   100
POL.   Affection? Pooh! You speak like a green girl,
Unsifted in such perilous circumstance.
Do you believe his tenders, as you call them?
OPH.   I do not know, my lord, what I should think.
POL.   Marry, I will teach you. Think yourself a baby   105
That you have ta'en these tenders for true pay
Which are not sterling. Tender yourself more dearly,
Or (not to crack the wind of the poor phrase,
Running it thus) you'll tender me a fool.
OPH.   My lord, he hath importuned me with love   110
In honorable fashion.
POL.   Ay, fashion you may call it. Go to, go to.
OPH.   And hath given countenance to his speech, my lord,
With almost all the holy vows of heaven.
POL.   Ay, springes to catch woodcocks. I do know,   115
When the blood burns, how prodigal the soul
Lends the tongue vows. These blazes, daughter,
Giving more light than heat, extinct in both
Even in their promise, as it is a-making,
You must not take for fire. From this time   120
Be something scanter of your maiden presence.

81. *season* ripen.   99. *tenders* offers.
83. *tend* attend, wait.   102. *Unsifted* untried.
90. *Marry* by Mary.   115. *springes* snares.

Set your entreatments at a higher rate
Than a command to parle. For Lord Hamlet,
Believe so much in him that he is young,
And with a larger tether may he walk   125
Than may be given you. In few, Ophelia,
Do not believe his vows, for they are brokers,
Not of that dye which their investments show,
But mere implorators of unholy suits,
Breathing like sanctified and pious bawds,   130
The better to beguile. This is for all:
I would not, in plain terms, from this time forth
Have you so slander any moment leisure
As to give words or talk with the Lord Hamlet.
Look to't, I charge you. Come your ways.   135
OPH.   I shall obey, my lord.   *Exeunt.*

[I.iv]

    Enter HAMLET, HORATIO *and* MARCELLUS.
HAM.   The air bites shrewdly; it is very cold.
HOR.   It is a nipping and an eager air.
HAM.   What hour now?
HOR.   I think it lacks of twelve.
MAR.   No, it is struck.
HOR.   Indeed? I heard it not. It then draws near the season   5
Wherein the spirit held his wont to walk.
           A flourish of trumpets, and two pieces go off.
What does this mean, my lord?
HAM.   The king doth wake to-night and takes his rouse,
Keeps wassail, and the swagg'ring up-spring reels,
And as he drains his draughts of Rhenish down,   10
The kettledrum and trumpet thus bray out
The triumph of his pledge.
HOR.   Is it a custom?
HAM.   Ay, marry, is't,
But to my mind, though I am native here
And to the manner born, it is a custom   15
More honored in the breach than the observance.
This heavy-headed revel east and west
Makes us traduced and taxed of other nations.
They clepe us drunkards, and with swinish phrase
Soil our addition, and indeed it takes   20

122. *entreatments* military negotiations for a surrender.
127. *brokers* go-betweens.
128. *investments* clothes.
129. *implorators* solicitors.

[I.iv] 2. *eager* sharp.
9. *wassail* carousal; *up-spring* a German dance.
18. *taxed of* censured by.
19. *clepe* call.
20. *addition* title added to a man's name to denote
his rank.

From our achievements, though performed at height,
The pith and marrow of our attribute.
So oft it chances in particular men,
That for some vicious mole of nature in them,
As in their birth, wherein they are not guilty   25
(Since nature cannot choose his origin),
By the o'ergrowth of some complexion,
Oft breaking down the pales and forts of reason,
Or by some habit that too much o'er-leavens
The form of plausive manners—that these men,   30
Carrying, I say, the stamp of one defect,
Being nature's livery or fortune's star,
His virtues else, be they as pure as grace,
As infinite as man may undergo,
Shall in the general censure take corruption   35
From that particular fault. The dram of evil
Doth all the noble substance often doubt
To his own scandal.

       Enter GHOST.

HOR.   Look, my lord, it comes.
HAM.   Angels and ministers of grace defend us!
Be thou a spirit of health or goblin damned,   40
Bring with thee airs from heaven or blasts from hell,
Be thy intents wicked or charitable,
Thou com'st in such a questionable shape
That I will speak to thee. I'll call thee Hamlet,
King, father, royal Dane. O, answer me!   45
Let me not burst in ignorance, but tell
Why thy canonized bones, hearséd in death,
Have burst their cerements; why the sepulchre
Wherein we saw thee quietly interred
Hath oped his ponderous and marble jaws   50
To cast thee up again. What may this mean
That thou, dead corse, again in complete steel
Revisits thus the glimpses of the moon,
Making night hideous, and we fools of nature
So horridly to shake our disposition   55
With thoughts beyond the reaches of our souls?
Say, why is this? wherefore? What should we do?
                     [GHOST] *beckons.*
HOR.   It beckons you to go away with it,

22. *attribute* reputation.
26. *his* its.
27. *complexion* one of the four temperaments
(sanguine, melancholy, choleric and phlegmatic).
29. *o'er-leavens* works change throughout.
30. *plausive* pleasing.

32. *livery* badge; *star* a person's fortune, rank, or
destiny, viewed as determined by the stars.
37. *doubt* put out, obliterate.
38. *his* its.
47. *canonized* buried according to the church's rule;
hearsed coffined, buried.

As if it some impartment did desire
To you alone.
MAR.   Look with what courteous action   60
It waves you to a more removéd ground.
But do not go with it.
HOR.   No, by no means.
HAM. It will not speak; then I will follow it.
HOR. Do not, my lord.
HAM.   Why, what should be the fear?
I do not set my life at a pin's fee,   65
And for my soul, what can it do to that,
Being a thing immortal as itself?
It waves me forth again. I'll follow it.
HOR. What if it tempt you toward the flood, my lord,
Or to the dreadful summit of the cliff   70
That beetles o'er his base into the sea,
And there assume some other horrible form,
Which might deprive your sovereignty of reason
And draw you into madness? Think of it.
The very place puts toys of desperation,   75
Without more motive, into every brain
That looks so many fathoms to the sea
And hears it roar beneath.
HAM.   It waves me still.
Go on. I'll follow thee.
MAR. You shall not go, my lord.
HAM.   Hold off your hands.   80
HOR. Be ruled, You shall not go.
HAM.   My fate cries out
And makes each petty artere in this body
As hardy as the Nemean lion's nerve.
Still am I called. Unhand me, gentlemen.
By heaven, I'll make a ghost of him that lets me.   85
I say, away!—Go on. I'll follow thee.
                        [*Exeunt*] GHOST *and* HAMLET.
HOR. He waxes desperate with imagination.
MAR. Let's follow. 'Tis not fit thus to obey him.
HOR. Have after. To what issue will this come?
MAR. Something is rotten in the state of Denmark.   90
HOR. Heaven will direct it.
MAR.   Nay, let's follow him.   *Exeunt*.

---

59. *impartment* communication.
71. *beetles* juts out.
73. *sovereignty of reason* state of being ruled by reason.
75. *toys* fancies, impules.

82. *artere* artery.
83. *Nemean lion* slain by Hercules in the performance of one of his twelve labors.
85. *lets* hinders.

[I.v]

Enter GHOST *and* HAMLET.
HAM.   Whither wilt thou lead me? Speak. I'll go no further.
GHOST.   Mark me.
HAM.   I will.
GHOST.   My hour is almost come
    When I to sulph'rous and tormenting flames
    Must render up myself.
HAM.   Alas, poor ghost!
GHOST.   Pity me not, but lend thy serious hearing   5
    To what I shall unfold.
HAM.   Speak. I am bound to hear.
GHOST.   So art thou to revenge, when thou shalt hear.
HAM.   What?
GHOST.   I am thy father's spirit,
    Doomed for a certain term to walk the night,   10
    And for the day confined to fast in fires,
    Till the foul crimes done in my days of nature
    Are burnt and purged away. But that I am forbid
    To tell the secrets of my prison house,
    I could a tale unfold whose lightest word   15
    Would harrow up thy soul, freeze thy young blood,
    Make thy two eyes like stars start from their spheres,
    Thy knotted and combinéd locks to part,
    And each particular hair to stand an end,
    Like quills upon the fretful porpentine.   20
    But this eternal blazon must not be
    To ears of flesh and blood. List, list, O, list!
    If thou didst ever thy dear father love—
HAM.   O God!
GHOST.   Revenge his foul and most unnatural murder.   25
HAM.   Murder!
GHOST.   Murder most foul, as in the best it is,
    But this most foul, strange, and unnatural.
HAM.   Haste me to know't, that I, with wings as swift
    As meditation or the thoughts of love,   30
    May sweep to my revenge.
GHOST.   I find thee apt,
    And duller shouldst thou be than the fat weed
    That roots itself in ease on Lethe wharf,
    Wouldst thou not stir in this. Now, Hamlet, hear.
    'Tis given out that, sleeping in my orchard,   35
    A serpent stung me. So the whole ear of Denmark

[I.v] 19. *an* on.   eternity.
20. *porpentine* porcupine.   33. *Lethe* the river in Hades that brings forgetful-
21. *eternal blazon* proclamation of the secrets of   ness.

Is by a forgéd process of my death
Rankly abused. But know, thou noble youth,
The serpent that did sting thy father's life
Now wears his crown.
HAM.   O my prophetic soul!   40
My uncle!
GHOST.   Ay, that incestuous, that adulterate beast,
With witchcraft of his wits, with traitorous gifts—
O wicked wit and gifts that have the power
So to seduce!—won to his shameful lust   45
The will of my most seeming virtuous queen.
O Hamlet, what a falling off was there,
From me, whose love was of that dignity
That it went hand in hand even with the vow
I made to her in marriage, and to decline   50
Upon a wretch whose natural gifts were poor
To those of mine!
But virtue, as it never will be moved,
Though lewdness court it in a shape of heaven,
So lust, though to a radiant angel linked,   55
Will sate itself in a celestial bed
And prey on garbage.
But soft, methinks I scent the morning air.
Brief let me be. Sleeping within my orchard,
My custom always of the afternoon,   60
Upon my secure hour thy uncle stole,
With juice of cursed hebona in a vial,
And in the porches of my ears did pour
The leperous distilment, whose effect
Holds such an enmity with blood of man   65
That swift as quicksilver it courses through
The natural gates and alleys of the body,
And with a sudden vigor it doth posset
And curd, like eager droppings into milk,
The thin and wholesome blood. So did it mine,   70
And a most instant tetter barked about
Most lazar-like with vile and loathsome crust
All my smooth body.
Thus was I sleeping by a brother's hand
Of life, of crown, of queen at once dispatched,   75
Cut off even in the blossoms of my sin,
Unhouseled, disappointed, unaneled,

37. *process* account.
61. *secure* free from suspicion.
62. *hebona* an imaginary poison, associated with henbane.
68. *posset* curdle.
69. *eager* acid.

71. *tetter* a skin eruption; *barked* covered as with bark.
77. *Unhouseled* without having received the sacrament; *disappointed* unprepared; *unaneled* without extreme unction.

No reck'ning made, but sent to my account
With all my imperfections on my head.
O, horrible! O, horrible! most horrible!   80
If thou hast nature in thee, bear it not.
Let not the royal bed of Denmark be
A couch for luxury and damnéd incest.
But howsomever thou pursues this act,
Taint not thy mind, nor let thy soul contrive   85
Against thy mother aught. Leave her to heaven,
And to those thorns that in her bosom lodge
To prick and sting her. Fare thee well at once.
The glowworm shows the matin to be near,
And gins to pale his uneffectual fire.   90
Adieu, adieu, adieu. Remember me.   [*Exit.*]

HAM.   O all you host of heaven! O earth! What else?
And shall I couple hell? O, fie! Hold, hold, my heart,
And you, my sinews, grow not instant old,
But bear me stiffly up. Remember thee?   95
Ay, thou poor ghost, whiles memory holds a seat
In this distracted globe. Remember thee?
Yea, from the table of my memory
I'll wipe away all trivial fond records,
All saws of books, all forms, all pressures past   100
That youth and observation copied there,
And thy commandment all alone shall live
Within the book and volume of my brain,
Unmixed with baser matter. Yes, by heaven!
O most pernicious woman!   105
O villain, villain, smiling, damnéd villain!
My tables—meet it is I set it down
That one may smile, and smile, and be a villain.
At least I am sure it may be so in Denmark.   [*Writing.*]
So, uncle, there you are. Now to my word: 110
It is 'Adieu, adieu. Remember me.'
I have sworn't.

            Enter HORATIO *and* MARCELLUS.
HOR.   My lord, my lord!
MAR.   Lord Hamlet!
HOR.   Heavens secure him!
HAM.   So be it!
MAR.   Illo, ho, ho, my lord!   115
HAM.   Hillo, ho, ho, boy! Come, bird, come.

---

83. *luxury* lust.
89. *matin* morning.
97. *globe* head.
98. *table* writing tablet, memorandum book (as at
line 107, below; here metaphorically of the mind).

99. *fond* foolish.
100. *saws* sayings; *forms* concepts; *pressures*
impressions.
115. *Illo, ho, ho* cry of the falconer to summon
his hawk.

MAR.   How is't, my noble lord?
HOR.   What news, my lord?
HAM.   O, wonderful!
HOR.   Good my lord, tell it.
HAM.   No, you will reveal it.
HOR.   Not I, my lord, by heaven.
MAR.   Nor I, my lord.   120
HAM.   How say you then, would heart of man once think it?
     But you'll be secret?
BOTH.   Ay, by heaven, my lord.
HAM.   There's never a villain dwelling in all Denmark
     But he's an arrant knave.
HOR.   There needs no ghost, my lord, come from the grave   125
     To tell us this.
HAM.   Why, right, you are in the right,
     And so without more circumstance at all
     I hold it fit that we shake hands and part,
     You, as your business and desire shall point you,
     For every man hath business and desire   130
     Such as it is, and for my own poor part,
     I will go pray.
HOR.   These are but wild and whirling words, my lord.
HAM.   I am sorry they offend you, heartily;
     Yes, faith, heartily.
HOR.   There's no offence, my lord.   135
HAM.   Yes, by Saint Patrick, but there is, Horatio,
     And much offence too. Touching this vision here,
     It is an honest ghost, that let me tell you.
     For your desire to know what is between us,
     O'ermaster't as you may. And now, good friends,   140
     As you are friends, scholars, and soldiers,
     Give me one poor request.
HOR.   What is't, my lord? We will.
HAM.   Never make known what you have seen to-night.
BOTH.   My lord, we will not.
HAM.   Nay, but swear't.
HOR.   In faith,   145
     My lord, not I.
MAR.   Nor I, my lord, in faith.
HAM.   Upon my sword.
MAR.   We have sworn, my lord, already.
HAM.   Indeed, upon my sword, indeed.
                     Ghost cries under the stage.
GHOST.   Swear.
HAM.   Ha, ha, boy, say'st thou so? Art thou there, truepenny?

136. *Saint Patrick* associated, in the late middle   sumably come.
ages, with purgatory, whence the ghost has pre-   149. *truepenny* honest fellow.

Come on. You hear this fellow in the cellarage.   150
Consent to swear.
HOR.   Propose the oath, my lord.
HAM.   Never to speak of this that you have seen,
Swear by my sword.
GHOST.   [*Beneath.*] Swear.
HAM.   Hic et ubique? Then we'll shift our ground.   155
Come hither, gentlemen,
And lay your hands again upon my sword.
Swear by my sword
Never to speak of this that you have heard.
GHOST.   [*Beneath.*] Swear by his sword.   160
HAM.   Well said, old mole! Canst work i' th' earth so fast?
A worthy pioneer! Once more remove, good friends.
HOR.   O day and night, but this is wondrous strange!
HAM.   And therefore as a stranger give it welcome.
There are more things in heaven and earth, Horatio,   165
Than are dreamt of in your philosophy.
But come.
Here as before, never, so help you mercy,
How strange or odd some'er I bear myself
(As I perchance hereafter shall think meet   170
To put an antic disposition on),
That you, at such times, seeing me, never shall,
With arms encumbered thus, or this head-shake,
Or by pronouncing of some doubtful phrase,
As 'Well, well, we know', or 'We could, and if we would'   175
Or 'If we list to speak', or 'There be, and if they might'
Or such ambiguous giving out, to note
That you know aught of me—this do swear,
So grace and mercy at your most need help you.
GHOST.   [*Beneath.*] Swear.   180
HAM.   Rest, rest, perturbéd spirit! So, gentlemen,
With all my love I do commend me to you,
And what so poor a man as Hamlet is
May do t'express his love and friending to you,
God willing, shall not lack. Let us go in together,   185
And still your fingers on your lips, I pray.
The time is out of joint. [O curséd spite
That ever I was born to set it right!]
Nay, come, let's go together.   *Exeunt.*

155. *Hic et ubique* here and everywhere.   171. *antic* mad.
162. *pioneer* miner.   173. *encumbered* folded.

[II.i]

Enter old POLONIUS, *with his man* [REYNALDO].
POL. Give him this money and these notes, Reynaldo.
REY. I will, my lord.
POL. You shall do marvellous wisely, good Reynaldo,
    Before you visit him, to make inquire
    Of his behavior.
REY.   My lord, I did intend it.   5
POL. Marry, well said, very well said. Look you, sir,
    Enquire me first what Danskers are in Paris,
    And how, and who, what means, and where they keep,
    What company, at what expense; and finding
    By this encompassment and drift of question   10
    That they do know my son, come you more nearer
    Than your particular demands will touch it.
    Take you as 'twere some distant knowledge of him,
    As thus, 'I know his father and his friends,
    And in part him'. Do you mark this, Reynaldo?   15
REY. Ay, very well, my lord.
POL. 'And in part him, but', you may say, 'not well,
    But if 't be he I mean, he's very wild,
    Addicted so and so'. And there put on him
    What forgeries you please; marry, none so rank   20
    As may dishonour him. Take heed of that.
    But, sir, such wanton, wild, and usual slips
    As are companions noted and most known
    To youth and liberty.
REY.   As gaming, my lord?
POL. Ay, or drinking, fencing, swearing, quarrelling,   25
    Drabbing—you may go so far.
REY. My lord, that would dishonor him.
POL. Faith, no, as you may season it in the charge.
    You must not put another scandal on him,
    That he is open to incontinency.   30
    That's not my meaning. But breathe his faults so quaintly
    That they may seem the taints of liberty,
    The flash and outbreak of a fiery mind,
    A savageness in unreclaiméd blood,
    Of general assault.
REY.   But, my good lord—   35
POL. Wherefore should you do this?

[II.i] 7. *Danskers* Danes.   26. *Drabbing* whoring.
8. *means* wealth.   28. *season* moderate.
10. *encompassment* talking round the matter. 31. *quaintly* delicately.
20. *forgeries* invented wrongdoings.   34. *unreclaimed* untamed.
24. *liberty* license.   35. *Of general assault* assailing all.

REY.   Ay, my lord,
I would know that.
POL.   Marry, sir, here's my drift,
And I believe it is a fetch of warrant.
You laying these slight sallies on my son,
As 'twere a thing a little soiled i' th' working,   40
Mark you,
Your party in converse, him you would sound,
Having ever seen in the prenominate crimes
The youth you breathe of guilty, be assured
He closes with you in this consequence,   45
'Good sir', or so, or 'friend', or 'gentleman',
According to the phrase or the addition
Of man and country.
REY.   Very good, my lord.
POL.   And then, sir, does 'a this—'a does—What was I about to
say?
By the mass, I was about to say something.   50
Where did I leave?
REY.   At 'closes in the consequence'.
POL.   At 'closes in the consequence'—ay, marry,
He closes thus: 'I know the gentleman.
I saw him yesterday, or th' other day,   55
Or then, or then, with such, or such, and as you say,
There was 'a gaming, there o'ertook in's rouse,
There falling out at tennis', or perchance
'I saw him enter such a house of sale',
Videlicet, a brothel, or so forth.   60
See you, now—
Your bait of falsehood takes this carp of truth,
And thus do we of wisdom and of reach,
With windlasses and with assays of bias,
By indirections find directions out;   65
So by my former lecture and advice
Shall you my son. You have me, have you not?
REY.   My lord, I have.
POL.   God buy ye; fare ye well.
REY.   Good my lord.
POL.   Observe his inclination in yourself.   70
REY.   I shall, my lord.
POL.   And let him ply his music.
REY.   Well, my lord.
POL.   Farewell.   *Exit* REYNALDO.

38. *fetch of warrant* allowable device.
43. *prenominate* before-named.
45. *closes* agrees; *in this consequence* as follows.
47. *addition* title.
60. *Videlicet* namely.

63. *reach* ability.
64. *windlasses* roundabout approaches; *assays of bias* indirect attempts.
68. *God buy ye* God be with you.

Enter OPHELIA.

How now, Ophelia, what's the matter?

OPH. O my lord, my lord, I have been so affrighted!

POL. With what, i' th' name of God?   75

OPH. My lord, as I was sewing in my closet,
Lord Hamlet with his doublet all unbraced,
No hat upon his head, his stockings fouled,
Ungartered and down-gyvéd to his ankle,
Pale as his shirt, his knees knocking each other,   80
And with a look so piteous in purport
As if he had been looséd out of hell
To speak of horrors—he comes before me.

POL. Mad for thy love?

OPH.   My lord, I do not know,
But truly I do fear it.

POL.   What said he?   85

OPH. He took me by the wrist, and held me hard,
Then goes he to the length of all his arm,
And with his other hand thus o'er his brow,
He falls to such perusal of my face
As 'a would draw it. Long stayed he so.   90
At last, a little shaking of mine arm,
And thrice his head thus waving up and down,
He raised a sigh so piteous and profound
As it did seem to shatter all his bulk,
And end his being. That done, he lets me go,   95
And with his head over his shoulder turned
He seemed to find his way without his eyes,
For out adoors he went without their helps,
And to the last bended their light on me.

POL. Come, go with me. I will go seek the king.   100
This is the very ecstasy of love,
Whose violent property fordoes itself,
And leads the will to desperate undertakings
As oft as any passion under heaven
That does afflict our natures. I am sorry.   105
What, have you given him any hard words of late?

OPH. No, my good lord, but as you did command
I did repel his letters, and denied
His access to me.

POL.   That hath made him mad.
I am sorry that with better heed and judgment   110
I had not quoted him. I feared he did but trifle,

---

76. *closet* private room.
77. *unbraced* unlaced.
79. *down-gyved* hanging down, like gyves or fetters on a prisoner's ankles.

101. *ecstasy* madness.
102. *fordoes* detroys.
111. *quoted* observed.

And meant to wrack thee; but beshrew my jealousy.
By heaven, it is as proper to our age
To cast beyond ourselves in our opinions
As it is common for the younger sort   115
To lack discretion. Come, go we to the king.
This must be known, which being kept close, might move
More grief to hide than hate to utter love.
Come.   *Exeunt.*

[II.ii]

> *Flourish. Enter* KING *and* QUEEN, ROSENCRANTZ *and* GUIL-
> DENSTERN [*and* ATTENDANTS].

KING.   Welcome, dear Rosencrantz and Guildenstern.
Moreover that we much did long to see you,
The need we have to use you did provoke
Our hasty sending. Something have you heard
Of Hamlet's transformation—so call it,   5
Sith nor th' exterior nor the inward man
Resembles that it was. What it should be,
More than his father's death, that thus hath put him
So much from th' understanding of himself,
I cannot dream of. I entreat you both   10
That, being of so young days brought up with him,
And sith so neighboured to his youth and havior,
That you vouchsafe your rest here in our court
Some little time, so by your companies
To draw him on to pleasures, and to gather   15
So much as from occasion you may glean,
Whether aught to us unknown afflicts him thus,
That opened lies within our remedy.
QUEEN.   Good gentlemen, he hath much talked of you,
And sure I am two men there is not living   20
To whom he more adheres. If it will please you
To show us so much gentry and good will
As to expend your time with us awhile
For the supply and profit of our hope,
Your visitation shall receive such thanks   25
As fits a king's remembrance.
ROS.   Both your majesties
Might, by the sovereign power you have of us,
Put your dread pleasures more into command
Than to entreaty.
GUIL.   But we both obey,

---

112. *wrack* ruin.   [II.ii] 6. *Sith* since.
113. *proper to* characteristic of.   18. *opened* disclosed.
117. *close* secret; *move* cause.   22. *gentry* courtesy.

And here give up ourselves in the full bent   30
To lay our service freely at your feet,
To be commanded.
KING.   Thanks, Rosencrantz and gentle Guildenstern.
QUEEN.   Thanks, Guildenstern and gentle Rosencrantz.
And I beseech you instantly to visit   35
My too much changed son. Go, some of you,
And bring these gentlemen where Hamlet is.
GUIL.   Heavens make our presence and our practices
Pleasant and helpful to him!
QUEEN.   Ay, amen!
        Exeunt ROSENCRANTZ *and* GUILDENSTERN [*with some* ATTEN-
        DANTS].

        Enter POLONIUS.
POL.   Th' ambassadors from Norway, my good lord,   40
Are joyfully returned.
KING.   Thou still hast been the father of good news.
POL.   Have I, my lord? I assure my good liege,
I hold my duty as I hold my soul,
Both to my God and to my gracious king;   45
And I do think—or else this brain of mine
Hunts not the trail of policy so sure
As it hath used to do—that I have found
The very cause of Hamlet's lunacy.
KING.   O, speak of that, that do I long to hear.   50
POL.   Give first admittance to th' ambassadors.
My news shall be the fruit to that great feast.
KING.   Thyself do grace to them, and bring them in.
                                        [*Exit* POLONIUS.]
He tells me, my dear Gertrude, he hath found
The head and source of all your son's distemper.   55
QUEEN.   I doubt it is no other but the main,
His father's death and our o'erhasty marriage.
KING.   Well, we shall sift him.

        Enter Ambassadors [(VOLTEMAND *and* CORNELIUS), *with* PO-
        LONIUS].
                                Welcome, my good friends,
Say, Voltemand, what from our brother Norway?
VOL.   Most fair return of greetings and desires.   60
Upon our first, he sent out to suppress
His nephew's levies, which to him appeared
To be a preparation 'gainst the Polack,
But better looked into, he truly found
It was against your highness, whereat grieved,   65

42. *still* ever.   63. *the Polack* the Polish nation.
56. *doubt* suspect.

That so his sickness, age, and impotence
Was falsely borne in hand, sends out arrests
On Fortinbras, which he in brief obeys,
Receives rebuke from Norway, and in fine,
Makes vow before his uncle never more   70
To give th' assay of arms against your majesty.
Whereon old Norway, overcome with joy,
Gives him threescore thousand crowns in annual fee,
And his commission to employ those soldiers,
So levied as before, against the Polack,   75
With an entreaty, herein further shown,   [*Gives a paper.*]
That it might please you to give quiet pass
Through your dominions for this enterprise,
On such regards of safety and allowance
As therein are set down.
KING.   It likes us well,   80
And at our more considered time we'll read,
Answer, and think upon this business.
Meantime we thank you for your well-took labor.
Go to your rest; at night we'll feast together.
Most welcome home!   *Exeunt* AMBASSADORS.
POL.   This business is well ended.   85
My liege and madam, to expostulate
What majesty should be, what duty is,
Why day is day, night night, and time is time,
Were nothing but to waste night, day, and time.
Therefore, since brevity is the soul of wit,   90
And tediousness the limbs and outward flourishes,
I will be brief. Your noble son is mad.
Mad call I it, for to define true madness,
What is't but to be nothing else but mad?
But let that go.
QUEEN.   More matter with less art.   95
POL.   Madam, I swear I use no art at all.
That he is mad, 'tis true: 'tis true 'tis pity,
And pity 'tis 'tis true. A foolish figure,
But farewell it, for I will use no art.
Mad let us grant him, then, and now remains   100
That we find out the cause of this effect,
Or rather say the cause of this defect,
For this effect defective comes by cause.
Thus it remains, and the remainder thus.
Perpend.   105

67. *borne in hand* deceived.   90. *wit* understanding.
69. *in fine* in the end.   95. *matter* meaning, sense.
71. *assay* trial.   105. *Perpend* consider.
79. *regards* considerations.

I have a daughter—have while she is mine—
Who in her duty and obedience, mark,
Hath given me this. Now gather, and surmise.   [Reads.]
  'To the celestial, and my soul's idol, the most beautified
Ophelia.'—That's an ill phrase, a vile phrase, 'beautified' is a 110
vile phrase. But you shall hear. Thus: [Reads.]
  'In her excellent white bosom, these, etc.'
QUEEN.   Came this from Hamlet to her?
POL.   Good madam, stay awhile. I will be faithful.

[Reads Letter.]

'Doubt thou the stars are fire,   115
  Doubt that the sun doth move;
Doubt truth to be a liar;
But never doubt I love.

O dear Ophelia, I am ill at these numbers. I have not art
to reckon my groans, but that I love thee best, O most best, be- 120
lieve it. Adieu.

Thine evermore, most dear lady, whilst
  this machine is to him, HAMLET.'
This in obedience hath my daughter shown me,
And more above, hath his solicitings,   125
As they fell out by time, by means, and place,
All given to mine ear.
KING.   But how hath she
Received his love?
POL.   What do you think of me?
KING.   As of a man faithful and honorable.
POL.   I would fain prove so. But what might you think,   130
When I had seen this hot love on the wing,
(As I perceived it, I must tell you that,
Before my daughter told me), what might you,
Or my dear majesty your queen here, think,
If I had played the desk or table-book,   135
Or given my heart a winking, mute and dumb,
Or looked upon this love with idle sight,
What might you think? No, I went round to work,
And my young mistress thus I did bespeak:
'Lord Hamlet is a prince out of thy star.   140
This must not be'. And then I prescripts gave her,
That she should lock herself from his resort,
Admit no messengers, receive no tokens.
Which done, she took the fruits of my advice;
And he repelled, a short tale to make,   145

119. *numbers* verses.   between.
123. machine body.   138. *round* directly.
135. *played . . . table-book* acted as silent go-

Fell into a sadness, then into a fast,
Thence to a watch, thence into a weakness,
Thence to a lightness, and by this declension,
Into the madness wherein now he raves,
And all we mourn for.
KING.   Do you think 'tis this?   150
QUEEN.   It may be, very like.
POL.   Hath there been such a time—I would fain know that—
That I have positively said ''Tis so',
When it proved otherwise?
KING.   Not that I know.
POL.   [*Pointing to his head and shoulder.*] Take this from this,
if this be otherwise.   155
If circumstances lead me, I will find
Where truth is hid, though it were hid indeed
Within the centre.
KING.   How may we try it further?
POL.   You know sometimes he walks four hours together
Here in the lobby.
QUEEN.   So he does, indeed.   160
POL.   At such a time I'll loose my daughter to him.
Be you and I behind an arras then.
Mark the encounter. If he love her not,
And be not from his reason fall'n thereon,
Let me be no assistant for a state,   165
But keep a farm and carters.
KING.   We will try it.

        Enter HAMLET [*reading on a book*].
QUEEN.   But look where sadly the poor wretch comes reading.
POL.   Away, I do beseech you both away,
I'll board him presently.
            [*Exeunt*] KING *and* QUEEN [*with* ATTENDANTS].
            O, give me leave,
How does my good Lord Hamlet?   170
HAM.   Well, God-a-mercy.
POL.   Do you know me, my lord?
HAM.   Excellent well, you are a fishmonger.
POL.   Not I, my lord.
HAM.   Then I would you were so honest a man.   175
POL.   Honest, my lord?
HAM.   Ay, sir, to be honest as this world goes, is to be one man
picked out of ten thousand.
POL.   That's very true, my lord.

147. *watch* sleeplessness.
148. *lightness* lightheadedness.
158. *centre* centre of the earth and of the Ptole-
maic universe.
169. *board* accost; *presently* immediately.

HAM.   For if the sun breed maggots in a dead dog, being a good 180
kissing carrion—Have you a daughter?

POL.   I have, my lord.

HAM.   Let her not walk i' th' sun. Conception is a blessing, but as
your daughter may conceive—friend, look to't.

POL.   [Aside.] How say you by that? Still harping on my daughter. 185
Yet he knew me not at first. 'A said I was a fishmonger. 'A is far
gone. And truly in my youth I suffered much extremity for love,
very near this. I'll speak to him again.—What do you read, my
lord?

HAM.   Words, words, words.   190

POL.   What is the matter, my lord?

HAM.   Between who?

POL.   I mean the matter that you read, my lord.

HAM.   Slanders, sir; for the satirical rogue says here that old men
have grey beards, that their faces are wrinkled, their eyes purging 195
thick amber and plum-tree gum, and that they have a plentiful
lack of wit, together with most weak hams—all which, sir, though
I most powerfully and potently believe, yet I hold it not honesty to
have it thus set down, for yourself, sir, shall grow old as I am, if
like a crab you could go backward.   200

POL.   [Aside.] Though this be madness, yet there is method in't.—
Will you walk out of the air, my lord?

HAM.   Into my grave?

POL.   [Aside.] Indeed, that's out of the air. How pregnant sometimes his replies are! a happiness that often madness hits on, which 205
reason and sanity could not so prosperously be delivered of. I will
leave him, and suddenly contrive the means of meeting between
him and my daughter.—My lord, I will take my leave of you.

HAM.   You cannot take from me anything that I will not more
willingly part withal—except my life, except my life, except my 210
life.

          Enter GUILDENSTERN and ROSENCRANTZ.

POL.   Fare you well, my lord.

HAM.   These tedious old fools!

POL.   You go to seek the Lord Hamlet. There he is.

ROS.   [To POLONIUS.] God save you, sir!   [Exit POLONIUS.] 215

GUIL.   My honored lord!

ROS.   My most dear lord!

HAM.   My excellent good friends! How dost thou, Guildenstern?
Ah, Rosencrantz! Good lads, how do you both?

ROS.   As the indifferent children of the earth.   220

GUIL.   Happy in that we are not over-happy;
On Fortune's cap we are not the very button.

---

204. *pregnant* full of meaning.
205. *happiness* aptness.

220. *indifferent* average.
222. *button* knob on the top of a cap.

HAM. Nor the soles of her shoe?

ROS. Neither, my lord.

HAM. Then you live about her waist, or in the middle of her 225
favors.

GUIL. Faith, her privates we.

HAM. In the secret parts of Fortune? O, most true, she is a strumpet.
What news?

ROS. None, my lord, but that the world's grown honest.   230

HAM. Then is doomsday near. But your news is not true. Let me
question more in particular. What have you, my good friends,
deserved at the hands of Fortune, that she sends you to prison
hither?

GUIL. Prison, my lord?   235

HAM. Denmark's a prison.

ROS. Then is the world one.

HAM. A goodly one, in which there are many confines, wards, and
dungeons, Denmark being one o' th' worst.

ROS. We think not so, my lord.   240

HAM. Why then 'tis none to you; for there is nothing either good or
bad, but thinking makes it so. To me it is a prison.

ROS. Why then your ambition makes it one. 'Tis too narrow for
your mind.

HAM. O God, I could be bounded in a nutshell and count myself 245
a king of infinite space, were it not that I have bad dreams.

GUIL. Which dreams indeed are ambition; for the very substance of
the ambitious is merely the shadow of a dream.

HAM. A dream itself is but a shadow.

ROS. Truly, and I hold ambition of so airy and light a quality that it 250
is but a shadow's shadow.

HAM. Then are our beggars bodies, and our monarchs and out-
stretched heroes the beggars' shadows. Shall we to th' court? for,
by my fay, I cannot reason.

BOTH. We'll wait upon you.   255

HAM. No such matter. I will not sort you with the rest of my servants; for to speak to you like an honest man, I am most dreadfully
attended. But in the beaten way of friendship, what make you at
Elsinore?

ROS. To visit you, my lord; no other occasion.   260

HAM. Beggar that I am, I am even poor in thanks, but I thank you;
and sure, dear friends, my thanks are too dear a halfpenny. Were
you not sent for? Is it your own inclining? Is it a free visitation?
Come, come, deal justly with me. Come, come, nay speak.

GUIL. What should we say, my lord?   265

HAM. Anything but to th' purpose. You were sent for, and there is
a kind of confession in your looks, which your modesties have not

---

254. *fay* faith.   256. *sort you with* put you in the same class with.

craft enough to color. I know the good king and queen have sent
for you.

ROS.   To what end, my lord?   270

HAM.   That you must teach me. But let me conjure you by the rights
of our fellowship, by the consonancy of our youth, by the obligation of our ever-preserved love, and by what more dear a better
proposer can charge you withal, be even and direct with me whether
you were sent for or no.   275

ROS.   [Aside to GUILDENSTERN.] What say you?

HAM.   [Aside.] Nay, then, I have an eye of you.—If you love me,
hold not off.

GUIL.   My lord, we were sent for.

HAM.   I will tell you why; so shall my anticipation prevent your   280
discovery, and your secrecy to the king and queen moult no feather.
I have of late—but wherefore I know not—lost all my mirth, for-
gone all custom of exercises; and indeed it goes so heavily with my
disposition, that this goodly frame the earth seems to me a sterile
promontory, this most excellent canopy the air, look you, this brave   285
o'er-hanging firmament, this majestical roof fretted with golden
fire, why it appeareth nothing to me but a foul and pestilent con-
gregation of vapors. What a piece of work is a man, how noble in
reason, how infinite in faculties, in form and moving, how express
and admirable in action, how like an angel in apprehension, how   290
like a god: the beauty of the world, the paragon of animals. And
yet to me, what is this quintessence of dust? Man delights not me,
nor woman neither, though by your smiling you seem to say so.

ROS.   My lord, there was no such stuff in my thoughts.

HAM.   Why did ye laugh, then, when I said 'Man delights not   295
me'?

ROS.   To think, my lord, if you delight not in man, what lenten
entertainment the players shall receive from you. We coted them
on the way, and hither are they coming to offer you service.

HAM.   He that plays the king shall be welcome—his majesty shall   300
have tribute on me; the adventurous knight shall use his foil and
target; the lover shall not sigh gratis; the humorous man shall end
his part in peace; the clown shall make those laugh whose lungs
are tickle o' th' sere; and the lady shall say her mind freely, or the
blank verse shall halt for't. What players are they?   305

ROS.   Even those you were wont to take such delight in, the trage-
dians of the city.

HAM.   How chances it they travel? Their residence, both in reputation and profit, was better both ways.

280. *prevent* forestall.
281. *discovery* disclosure.
286. *fretted* decorated with fretwork.
297. *lenten* scanty
298. *coted* passed.
301–2. *foil and target* spear and shield.
302. *humorous man* the actor who plays the ec-

centric character dominated by one of the four humors.
304. *tickle o' th' sere* easily set off (*sere* is that part
of a gunlock which keeps the hammar at full or
half cock).
305. *halt* limp.

ROS.   I think their inhibition comes by the means of the late in- 310
novation.

HAM.   Do they hold the same estimation they did when I was in the
city? Are they so followed?

ROS.   No, indeed, are they not.

HAM.   How comes it? Do they grow rusty?   315

ROS.   Nay, their endeavor keeps in the wonted pace; but there
is, sir, an eyrie of children, little eyases, that cry out on the top of
question, and are most tyrannically clapped for't. These are now
the fashion, and so berattle the common stages (so they call them)
that many wearing rapiers are afraid of goose quills and dare 320
scarce come thither.

HAM.   What, are they children? Who maintains 'em? How are
they escoted? Will they pursue the quality no longer than they can
sing? Will they not say afterwards, if they should grow themselves
to common players (as it is most like, if their means are no better), 325
their writers do them wrong to make them exclaim against their
own succession?

ROS.   Faith, there has been much to do on both sides; and the nation holds it no sin to tarre them to controversy. There was for a
while no money bid for argument, unless the poet and the 330
player went to cuffs in the question.

HAM.   Is't possible?

GUIL.   O, there has been much throwing about of brains.

HAM.   Do the boys carry it away?

ROS.   Ay, that they do, my lord, Hercules and his load too.   335

HAM.   It is not very strange, for my uncle is King of Denmark, and
those that would make mouths at him while my father lived give
twenty, forty, fifty, a hundred ducats apiece for his picture in little.
'Sblood, there is something in this more than natural, if philosophy could find it out.   A flourish. 340

GUIL.   There are the players.

HAM.   Gentlemen, you are welcome to Elsinore. Your hands. Come
then, th' appurtenance of welcome is fashion and ceremony.

---

310. *inhibition* prohibition of plays by authority
(possibly with reference to decree of the Privy
Council of 22 June 1600, limiting the number of
London theater companies to two, and stipulating
that the two were to perform only twice a week);
innovation meaning uncertain (sometimes taken
to refer to the re-introduction, ca. 1600, on the
London theatrical scene of companies of boy actors performing in private theaters; sometimes in-
terpreted as "political upheaval," with special reference to Essex's rebellion, February, 1601).
317. *eyrie* nest; *eyases* nestling hawks (here, the
boys in the children's companies training as actors).
317–18. *on the top of question* louder than all
others on matter of dispute.

319. *common stages* public theaters of the *common players* (below, line 325), organized in companies composed mainly of adult actors.
320. *goose quills* pens (of the satiric dramatists
writing for the private theaters).
323. *escoted* maintained; *pursue the quality* continue in the profession of acting.
324. *sing* i.e., until their voices change.
329. *tarre* incite.
330. *argument* plot of a play.
335. *load* i.e., the world (the sign of the Globe
Theatre represented Hercules bearing the world on
his shoulders).
337. *mouths* grimaces.
338. *in little* in miniature.
343. *appurtenance* adjuncts.

Let me comply with you in this garb, lest my extent to the play- 345
ers, which I tell you must show fairly outwards, should more appear like entertainment than yours. You are welcome. But my
uncle-father and aunt-mother are deceived.
GUIL.   In what, my dear lord?
HAM.   I am but mad north-north-west; when the wind is southerly
I know a hawk from a handsaw.   350

                Enter POLONIUS.
POL.   Well be with you, gentlemen.
HAM.   Hark you, Guildenstern—and you too—at each ear a hearer.
That great baby you see there is not yet out of his swaddling clouts.
ROS.   Happily he is the second time come to them, for they say an
old man is twice a child.   355
HAM.   I will prophesy he comes to tell me of the players. Mark it.
—You say right, sir, a Monday morning, 'twas then indeed.
POL.   My lord, I have news to tell you.
HAM.   My lord, I have news to tell you.
When Roscius was an actor in Rome—   360
POL.   The actors are come hither, my lord.
HAM.   Buzz, buzz.
POL.   Upon my honor—
HAM.   Then came each actor on his ass—
POL.   The best actors in the world, either for tragedy, comedy, his- 365
tory, pastoral, pastoral-comical, historical-pastoral, tragical-histor-
ical, tragical-comical-historical-pastoral, scene individable, or poem
unlimited. Seneca cannot be too heavy nor Plautus too light. For
the law of writ and the liberty, these are the only men.
HAM.   O Jephthah, judge of Israel, what a treasure hadst thou!   370
POL.   What a treasure had he, my lord?
HAM.   Why—

            'One fair daughter, and no more,
            The which he loved passing well'.

POL.   [Aside.] Still on my daughter.   375
HAM.   Am I not i' th' right, old Jephthah?
POL.   If you call me Jephthah, my lord, I have a daughter that I love
passing well.

344. *extent* welcome.
350. *hawk* mattock or pickaxe (also called "hack," here used with a play on *hawk* as a bird); *handsaw* a saw managed with one hand (here used with a play on some corrupt form of *hernshaw*, "heron").
354. *Happily* perhaps.
360. *Roscius* the greatest of Roman comic actors, though regarded by the Elizabethans as a tragic one.
367. *scene individable* i.e., a play that observes the unities of time and place.
367–68. *poem unlimited* a play that does not observe the unities; *Seneca* Roman writer of tragedies; *Plautus* Roman comic dramatist.
369. *law of writ and the liberty* i.e., plays according to strict classical rules, and those that ignored the unities of time and place.
370. *Jephthah* was compelled to sacrifice a beloved daughter (Judges 11). Hamlet quotes from a contemporary ballad titled *Jephthah, Judge of Israel* at lines 373–74, 382, and 384.

HAM.   Nay, that follows not.
POL.   What follows then, my lord?   380
HAM.   Why—

            'As by lot, God wot'

and then, you know,

            'It came to pass, as most like it was.'

The first row of the pious chanson will show you more, for look 385
where my abridgement comes.

        Enter the PLAYERS.
You are welcome, masters; welcome, all.—I am glad to see thee
well.—Welcome, good friends.—O, old friend! Why thy face is
valanced since I saw thee last. Com'st thou to beard me in Denmark?—What, my young lady and mistress? By'r lady, your lady- 390
ship is nearer to heaven than when I saw you last by the altitude
of a chopine. Pray God your voice, like a piece of uncurrent gold,
be not cracked within the ring.—Masters, you are all welcome.
We'll e'en to't like French falconers, fly at anything we see. We'll
have a speech straight. Come give us a taste of your quality, come 395
a passionate speech.
1 PLAY.   What speech, my good lord?
HAM.   I heard thee speak me a speech once, but it was never
acted, or if it was, not above once, for the play, I remember, pleased
not the million; 'twas caviary to the general. But it was—as I re- 400
ceived it, and others whose judgments in such matters cried in the
top of mine—an excellent play, well digested in the scenes, set
down with as much modesty as cunning. I remember one said
there were no sallets in the lines to make the matter savory, nor no
matter in the phrase that might indict the author of affectation, but 405
called it an honest method, as wholesome as sweet, and by very
much more handsome than fine. One speech in't I chiefly loved.
'Twas Æneas' tale to Dido, and thereabout of it especially when
he speaks of Priam's slaughter. If it live in your memory, begin at
this line—let me see, let me see: 410

        'The rugged Pyrrhus, like th' Hyrcanian beast'—

        'tis not so; it begins with Pyrrhus—

---

385. *row* stanza.
389. *valanced* bearded.
390. *young lady* i.e., the boy who plays female
roles.
392. *chopine* a shoe with high cork heel and sole.
393. *cracked within the ring* a coin cracked within
the circle surrounding the head of the sovereign
was no longer legal tender and so *uncurrent.*

395. *straight* immediately.
400. *caviary* caviare; *general* multitude.
402. *digested* arranged.
404. *sallets* salads, highly seasoned passages.
407. *more handsome than fine* admirable rather
than appealing by mere cleverness.
411. *Hyrcanian beast* tiger.

'The rugged Pyrrhus, he whose sable arms,
Black as his purpose, did the night resemble
When he lay couchéd in th' ominous horse,   415
Hath now this dread and black complexion smeared
With heraldry more dismal; head to foot
Now is he total gules, horridly tricked
With blood of fathers, mothers, daughters, sons,
Baked and impasted with the parching streets,   420
That lend a tyrannous and a damnéd light
To their lord's murder. Roasted in wrath and fire,
And thus o'er-sizéd with coagulate gore,
With eyes like carbuncles, the hellish Pyrrhus
Old grandsire Priam seeks.'   425
     So proceed you.
POL.   Fore God, my lord, well spoken, with good accent and good
     discretion.
1 PLAY.   'Anon he finds him
Striking too short at Greeks. His antique sword,   430
Rebellious to his arm, lies where it falls,
Repugnant to command. Unequal matched,
Pyrrhus at Priam drives, in rage strikes wide.
But with the whiff and wind of his fell sword
Th' unnervéd father falls. Then senseless Ilium,   435
Seeming to feel this blow, with flaming top
Stoops to his base, and with a hideous crash
Takes prisoner Pyrrhus' ear. For, lo! his sword,
Which was declining on the milky head
Of reverend Priam, seemed i' th' air to stick.   440
So as a painted tyrant Pyrrhus stood,
And like a neutral to his will and matter,
Did nothing.
But as we often see, against some storm,
A silence in the heavens, the rack stand still,   445
The bold winds speechless, and the orb below
As hush as death, anon the dreadful thunder
Doth rend the region; so, after Pyrrhus' pause,
A rouséd vengeance sets him new awork,
And never did the Cyclops' hammers fall   450
On Mars's armor, forged for proof eterne,
With less remorse than Pyrrhus' bleeding sword
Now falls on Priam.

---

415. *horse* i.e., the Trojan horse.
418. *gules* heraldic term for red; *tricked* delineated.
423. *o'er-sized* covered as with size; *coagulate* clotted.
432. *Repugnant* refractory.
434. *fell* fierce, cruel.

444. *against* just before.
445. *rack* mass of cloud.
448. *region* air.
450. *Cyclops* giant workmen who made armor in the smithy of Vulcan.
451. *proof eterne* to be forever impenetrable.

Out, out, thou strumpet, Fortune! All you gods,
In general synod take away her power,   455
Break all the spokes and fellies from her wheel,
And bowl the round nave down the hill of heaven
As low as to the fiends.'
POL. This is too long.
HAM. It shall to the barber's with your beard.—Prithee say on. 460
He's for a jig, or a tale of bawdry, or he sleeps. Say on; come to
Hecuba.
1 PLAY. 'But who, ah woe! had seen the mobled queen—'
HAM. 'The mobled queen'?
POL. That's good.   465
1 PLAY. 'Run barefoot up and down, threat'ning the flames
With bisson rheum, a clout upon that head
Where late the diadem stood, and for a robe,
About her lank and all o'er-teeméd loins,
A blanket, in the alarm of fear caught up—   470
Who this had seen, with tongue in venom steeped,
'Gainst Fortune's state would treason have pronounced.
But if the gods themselves did see her then,
When she saw Pyrrhus make malicious sport
In mincing with his sword her husband's limbs,   475
The instant burst of clamor that she made,
Unless things mortal move them not at all,
Would have made milch the burning eyes of heaven,
And passion in the gods.'
POL. Look whe'r he has not turned his color, and has tears in's 480
eyes. Prithee no more.
HAM. 'Tis well. I'll have thee speak out the rest of this soon.—
Good my lord, will you see the players well bestowed? Do you
hear, let them be well used, for they are the abstract and brief
chronicles of the time; after your death you were better have a bad 485
epitaph than their ill report while you live.
POL. My lord, I will use them according to their desert.
HAM. God's bodkin, man, much better. Use every man after his
desert, and who shall 'scape whipping? Use them after your own
honor and dignity. The less they deserve, the more merit is in your 490
bounty. Take them in.
POL. Come, sirs.
HAM. Follow him, friends. We'll hear a play tomorrow. [Aside to
First Player.] Dost thou hear me, old friend, can you play 'The
Murder of Gonzago'?   495

---

456. *fellies* the curved pieces forming the rim of a
wheel.
457. *nave* hub of a wheel.
463. *mobled* muffled.
467. *bisson rheum* blinding tears.

469. *o'er-teemed* exhausted by many births.
472. *state* government.
478. *milch* moist, tearful (lit., milk-giving).
484. *abstract* summary account.
488. *God's bodkin* by God's dear body.

1 PLAY. Ay, my lord.
HAM. We'll ha't tomorrow night. You could for a need study a speech
  of some dozen or sixteen lines which I would set down and insert
  in't, could you not?
1 PLAY. Ay, my lord.   500
HAM. Very well. Follow that lord, and look you mock him not.
                              Exeunt POLONIUS *and* PLAYERS.
  My good friends, I'll leave you till night. You are welcome to
  Elsinore.
ROS. Good my lord. *Exeunt* [ROSENCRANTZ *and* GUILDENSTERN].
HAM. Ay, so God buy to you. Now I am alone.   505
  O, what a rogue and peasant slave am I!
  Is it not monstrous that this player here,
  But in a fiction, in a dream of passion,
  Could force his soul so to his own conceit
  That from her working all his visage wanned;   510
  Tears in his eyes, distraction in his aspect,
  A broken voice, and his whole function suiting
  With forms to his conceit? And all for nothing,
  For Hecuba!
  What's Hecuba to him or he to her,   515
  That he should weep for her? What would he do
  Had he the motive and the cue for passion
  That I have? He would drown the stage with tears,
  And cleave the general ear with horrid speech,
  Make mad the guilty, and appal the free,   520
  Confound the ignorant, and amaze indeed
  The very faculties of eyes and ears.
  Yet I,
  A dull and muddy-mettled rascal, peak
  Like John-a-dreams, unpregnant of my cause,   525
  And can say nothing; no, not for a king
  Upon whose property and most dear life
  A damned defeat was made. Am I a coward?
  Who calls me villain, breaks my pate across,
  Plucks off my beard and blows it in my face,   530
  Tweaks me by the nose, gives me the lie i' th' throat
  As deep as to the lungs? Who does me this?
  Ha, 'swounds, I should take it; for it cannot be
  But I am pigeon-livered and lack gall
  To make oppression bitter, or ere this   535
  I should 'a fatted all the region kites
  With this slave's offal. Bloody, bawdy villain!

509. *conceit* imagination.   525. *unpregnant* not quickened to action.
519. *general* public.   536. *region kites* kites of the air.
524. *muddy-mettled* dull-spirited; *peak* mope.

Remorseless, treacherous, lecherous, kindless villain!
Why, what an ass am I! This is most brave,
That I, the son of a dear father murdered,   540
Prompted to my revenge by heaven and hell,
Must like a whore unpack my heart with words,
And fall a-cursing like a very drab,
A scullion! Fie upon't! foh!
About, my brains. Hum—I have heard   545
That guilty creatures sitting at a play,
Have by the very cunning of the scene
Been struck so to the soul that presently
They have proclaimed their malefactions;
For murder, though it have no tongue, will speak   550
With most miraculous organ. I'll have these players
Play something like the murder of my father
Before mine uncle. I'll observe his looks.
I'll tent him to the quick. If 'a do blench,
I know my course. The spirit that I have seen   555
May be a devil, and the devil hath power
T' assume a pleasing shape, yea, and perhaps
Out of my weakness and my melancholy,
As he is very potent with such spirits,
Abuses me to damn me. I'll have grounds   560
More relative than this. The play's the thing
Wherein I'll catch the conscience of the king.   *Exit.*

[III.i]

      Enter KING, QUEEN, POLONIUS, OPHELIA, ROSENCRANTZ,
      GUILDENSTERN, LORDS.
KING.   And can you by no drift of conference
   Get from him why he puts on this confusion,
   Grating so harshly all his days of quiet
   With turbulent and dangerous lunacy?
ROS.   He does confess he feels himself distracted,   5
   But from what cause 'a will by no means speak.
GUIL.   Nor do we find him forward to be sounded,
   But with a crafty madness keeps aloof

---

538. *kindless* unnatural. Following this line, F adds the words "Oh Vengeance!" Their inappropriateness to the occasion is noted by Professor Harold Jenkins (in his "Playhouse Interpolations in the Folio Text of Hamlet," *Studies in Bibliography* 13 [1960]: 37). Professor Jenkins remarks that the folio text, by introducing Hamlet's "call for vengeance while he is still absorbed in self-reproaches, both anticipates and misconstrues" the crisis of his passion and of the speech, which comes in fact at line

545 ("About, my brains"), when "he abandons his self-reproaches and plans action."
544. *scullion* kitchen wench.
548. *presently* immediately.
554. *tent* probe; *blench* flinch.
560. *Abuses* deludes.
561. *relative* relevant.

[III.i] 7. *forward* willing.

When we would bring him on to some confession
Of his true state.
QUEEN.   Did he receive you well?   10
ROS.   Most like a gentleman.
GUIL.   But with much forcing of his disposition.
ROS.   Niggard of question, but of our demands
    Most free in his reply.
QUEEN.   Did you assay him
    To any pastime?   15
ROS.   Madam, it so fell out that certain players
    We o'er-raught on the way. Of these we told him,
    And there did seem in him a kind of joy
    To hear of it. They are here about the court,
    And as I think, they have already order   20
    This night to play before him.
POL.   'Tis most true,
    And he beseeched me to entreat your majesties
    To hear and see the matter.
KING.   With all my heart, and it doth much content me
    To hear him so inclined.   25
    Good gentlemen, give him a further edge,
    And drive his purpose into these delights.
ROS.   We shall, my lord. *Exeunt* ROSENCRANTZ *and* GUILDENSTERN.
KING.   Sweet Gertrude, leave us too,
    For we have closely sent for Hamlet hither,
    That he, as 'twere by accident, may here   30
    Affront Ophelia.
    Her father and myself (lawful espials)
    We'll so bestow ourselves that, seeing unseen,
    We may of their encounter frankly judge,
    And gather by him, as he is behaved,   35
    If't be th' affliction of his love or no
    That thus he suffers for.
QUEEN.   I shall obey you.—
    And for your part, Ophelia, I do wish
    That your good beauties be the happy cause
    Of Hamlet's wildness. So shall I hope your virtues   40
    Will bring him to his wonted way again,
    To both your honors.
OPH.   Madam, I wish it may.
                        [*Exit* QUEEN *with* LORDS.]
POL.   Ophelia, walk you here.—Gracious, so please you,
    We will bestow ourselves.—[*to* OPHELIA.] Read on this book,

14. *essay* try to win.   29. *closely* privately.
17. *o'er-raught* overtook.   31. *Affront* meet face to face.
26. *give him a further edge* sharpen his inclina-   32. *espials* spies.
tion.

That show of such an exercise may color   45
Your loneliness.—We are oft to blame in this,
'Tis too much proved, that with devotion's visage
And pious action we do sugar o'er
The devil himself.
KING.   [*Aside.*]   O, 'tis too true.
How smart a lash that speech doth give my conscience!   50
The harlot's cheek, beautied with plast'ring art,
Is not more ugly to the thing that helps it
Then is my deed to my most painted word.
O heavy burden!
POL.   I hear him coming. Let's withdraw, my lord.   55

                     [*Exeunt* KING *and* POLONIUS.]

     Enter HAMLET.
HAM.   To be, or not to be, that is the question:
Whether 'tis nobler in the mind to suffer
The slings and arrows of outrageous fortune,
Or to take arms against a sea of troubles,
And by opposing end them. To die, to sleep—   60
No more; and by a sleep to say we end
The heartache, and the thousand natural shocks
That flesh is heir to: 'tis a consummation
Devoutly to be wished. To die, to sleep—
To sleep, perchance to dream, ay there's the rub;   65
For in that sleep of death what dreams may come
When we have shuffled off this mortal coil
Must give us pause. There's the respect
That makes calamity of so long life:
For who would bear the whips and scorns of time,   70
Th' oppressor's wrong, the proud man's contumely,
The pangs of despised love, the law's delay,
The insolence of office, and the spurns
That patient merit of th' unworthy takes,
When he himself might his quietus make   75
With a bare bodkin? Who would fardels bear,
To grunt and sweat under a weary life,
But that the dread of something after death,
The undiscovered country, from whose bourn
No traveller returns, puzzles the will,   80
And makes us rather bear those ills we have
Than fly to others that we know not of?
Thus conscience does make cowards of us all,

---

45. *exercise* act of devotion; *color* give an appearance of naturalness to.
52. *to* compared to.
65. *rub* obstacle (lit., obstruction encountered by
bowler's ball).

67. *coil* bustle, turmoil.
75. *quietus* settlement.
76. *bodkin* dagger; *fardels* burdens.
79. *bourn* realm.

And thus the native hue of resolution
Is sicklied o'er with the pale cast of thought,   85
And enterprises of great pitch and moment
With this regard their currents turn awry
And lose the name of action. Soft you now,
The fair Ophelia.—Nymph, in thy orisons
Be all my sins remembered.
OPH.   Good my lord,   90
How does your honor for this many a day?
HAM.   I humbly thank you, well.
OPH.   My lord, I have remembrances of yours
That I have longed long to re-deliver.
I pray you now receive them.
HAM.   No, not I,   95
I never gave you aught.
OPH.   My honored lord, you know right well you did,
And with them words of so sweet breath composed
As made the things more rich. Their perfume lost,
Take these again, for to the noble mind   100
Rich gifts wax poor when givers prove unkind.
There, my lord.
HAM.   Ha, ha! are you honest?
OPH.   My lord?
HAM.   Are you fair?   105
OPH.   What means your lordship?
HAM.   That if you be honest and fair, your honesty should admit no
discourse to your beauty.
OPH.   Could beauty, my lord, have better commerce than with hon-
esty?   110
HAM.   Ay, truly, for the power of beauty will sooner transform hon-
esty from what it is to a bawd than the force of honesty can trans-
late beauty into his likeness. This was sometime a paradox, but
now the time gives it proof. I did love you once.
OPH.   Indeed, my lord, you made me believe so.   115
HAM.   You should not have believed me, for virtue cannot so inoculate our old stock but we shall relish of it. I loved you not.
OPH.   I was the more deceived.
HAM.   Get thee to a nunnery. Why wouldst thou be a breeder of
sinners? I am myself indifferent honest, but yet I could accuse me   120
of such things that it were better my mother had not borne me: I
am very proud, revengeful, ambitious, with more offences at my
beck than I have thoughts to put them in, imagination to give
them shape, or time to act them in. What should such fellows as
I do crawling between earth and heaven? We are arrant knaves all;   125

86. *pitch* height.   103. *honest* chaste.
87. *regard* consideration.   116–17. *inoculate* graft.
89. *orisons* prayers.   120. *indifferent honest* moderately respectable.

believe none of us. Go thy ways to a nunnery. Where's your father?

OPH.   At home, my lord.

HAM.   Let the doors be shut upon him, that he may play the fool
nowhere but in's own house. Farewell.   130

OPH.   O, help him, you sweet heavens!

HAM.   If thou dost marry, I'll give thee this plague for thy dowry:
be thou as chaste as ice, as pure as snow, thou shalt not escape   ·
calumny. Get thee to a nunnery, farewell. Or if thou wilt needs
marry, marry a fool, for wise men know well enough what mon-   135
sters you make of them. To a nunnery, go, and quickly too. Farewell.

OPH.   Heavenly powers, restore him!

HAM.   I have heard of your paintings well enough. God hath given
you one face, and you make yourselves another. You jig and am-   140
ble, and you lisp; you nickname God's creatures, and make your
wantonness your ignorance. Go to, I'll no more on't, it hath made
me mad. I say we will have no moe marriage. Those that are married already, all but one, shall live. The rest shall keep as they are.
To a nunnery, go.   *Exit.* 145

OPH.   O, what a noble mind is here o'erthrown!
The courtier's, soldier's, scholar's, eye, tongue, sword,
Th' expectancy and rose of the fair state,
The glass of fashion and the mould of form,
Th' observed of all observers, quite quite down!   150
And I of ladies most deject and wretched,
That sucked the honey of his musiced vows,
Now see that noble and most sovereign reason
Like sweet bells jangled, out of time and harsh;
That unmatched form and feature of blown youth   155
Blasted with ecstasy. O, woe is me
T' have seen what I have seen, see what I see!

         Enter KING *and* POLONIUS.

KING.   Love? His affections do not that way tend,
Nor what he spake, though it lacked form a little,
Was not like madness. There's something in his soul   160
O'er which his melancholy sits on brood,
And I do doubt the hatch and the disclose
Will be some danger; which for to prevent,
I have in quick determination
Thus set it down: he shall with speed to England   165
For the demand of our neglected tribute.

141–42. *make your wantonness your ignorance*
excuse your wanton behavior with the plea that
you don't know any better.
143. *moe* more.
148. *expectancy* hope.

149. *glass* mirror.
155. *blown* blooming.
156. *ecstasy* madness.
158. *affections* emotions.
162. *doubt* fear.

Haply the seas and countries different,
With variable objects, shall expel
This something-settled matter in his heart
Whereon his brains still beating puts him thus   170
From fashion of himself. What think you on't?
POL.   It shall do well. But yet do I believe
The origin and commencement of his grief
Sprung from neglected love.—How now, Ophelia?
You need not tell us what Lord Hamlet said,   175
We heard it all.—My lord, do as you please,
But if you hold it fit, after the play
Let his queen-mother all alone entreat him
To show his grief. Let her be round with him,
And I'll be placed, so please you, in the ear   180
Of all their conference. If she find him not,
To England send him; or confine him where
Your wisdom best shall think.
KING.   It shall be so.
Madness in great ones must not unwatched go.   *Exeunt.*

[III.ii]

        Enter HAMLET *and three of the* PLAYERS.
HAM.   Speak the speech, I pray you, as I pronounced it to you,
trippingly on the tongue; but if you mouth it as many of our players
do, I had as lief the town-crier spoke my lines. Nor do not saw the
air too much with your hand thus, but use all gently, for in the
very torrent, tempest, and as I may say, whirlwind of your passion,   5
you must acquire and beget a temperance that may give it smooth-
ness. O, it offends me to the soul to hear a robustious periwig-
pated fellow tear a passion to tatters, to very rags, to split the ears
of the groundlings, who for the most part are capable of nothing
but inexplicable dumb shows and noise. I would have such a fel-   10
low whipped for o'erdoing Termagant. It out-Herods Herod. Pray
you avoid it.
1 PLAY.   I warrant your honour.
HAM.   Be not too tame neither, but let your own discretion be your
tutor. Suit the action to the word, the word to the action, with this   15
special observance, that you o'erstep not the modesty of nature; for
anything so o'erdone is from the purpose of playing, whose end
both at the first, and now, was and is, to hold as 'twere the mirror
up to nature, to show virtue her own feature, scorn her own image,
and the very age and body of the time his form and pressure. Now   20

---

179. *round* plain-spoken.

[III.ii] 9. *groundlings* spectators who paid least and
stood on the ground.

11. *Termagant* thought to be a Mohammedan de-
ity, and represented in medieval mystery plays as a
violent and ranting personage; *Herod* represented
in the mystery plays as a blustering tyrant.

this overdone, or come tardy off, though it makes the unskilful
laugh, cannot but make the judicious grieve, the censure of the
which one must in your allowance o'erweigh a whole theatre of
others. O, there be players that I have seen play—and heard others
praise, and that highly—not to speak it profanely, that neither hav-   25
ing th' accent of Christians, nor the gait of Christian, pagan, nor
man, have so strutted and bellowed that I have thought some of
nature's journeymen had made men, and not made them well,
they imitated humanity so abominably.

1 PLAY.   I hope we have reformed that indifferently with us.   30

HAM.   O, reform it altogether. And let those that play your clowns
speak no more than is set down for them, for there be of them that
will themselves laugh, to set on some quantity of barren spectators
to laugh too, though in the meantime some necessary question of
the play be then to be considered. That's villainous, and shows a   35
most pitiful ambition in the fool that uses it. Go, make you
ready.   [*Exeunt* PLAYERS.]

Enter POLONIUS, GUILDENSTERN, *and* ROSENCRANTZ.

How now, my lord? Will the king hear this piece of work?

POL.   And the queen too, and that presently.

HAM.   Bid the players make haste.   [*Exit* POLONIUS.]   40
Will you two help to hasten them?

ROS.   Ay, my lord.   *Exeunt they two.*

HAM.   What, ho, Horatio!

Enter HORATIO.

HOR.   Here, sweet lord, at your service.

HAM.   Horatio, thou art e'en as just a man   45
As e'er my conversation coped withal.

HOR.   O my dear lord!

HAM.   Nay, do not think I flatter,
For what advancement may I hope from thee,
That no revenue hast but thy good spirits
To feed and clothe thee? Why should the poor be flattered?   50
No, let the candied tongue lick absurd pomp,
And crook the pregnant hinges of the knee
Where thrift may follow fawning. Dost thou hear?
Since my dear soul was mistress of her choice
And could of men distinguish her election,   55
S'hath sealed thee for herself, for thou hast been
As one in suff'ring all that suffers nothing,
A man that Fortune's buffets and rewards
Hast ta'en with equal thanks; and blest are those

22. *censure* judgment, opinion.   52. *pregnant* ready.
30. *indifferently* fairly well.   53. *thrift* profit.
46. *coped* encountered.   55. *election* choice.

Whose blood and judgment are so well comeddled   60
That they are not a pipe for Fortune's finger
To sound what stop she please.⌈Give me that man
That is not passion's slave, and I will wear him
In my heart's core, ay, in my heart of heart,
As I do thee.⌉Something too much of this.   65
There is a play to-night before the king.
One scene of it comes near the circumstance
Which I have told thee of my father's death.
I prithee, when thou seest that act afoot,
Even with the very comment of thy soul   70
Observe my uncle. If his occulted guilt
Do not itself unkennel in one speech,
It is a damnéd ghost that we have seen,
And my imaginations are as foul
As Vulcan's stithy. Give him heedful note,   75
For I mine eyes will rivet to his face,
And after we will both our judgments join
In censure of his seeming.
HOR.   Well, my lord.
If 'a steal aught the whilst this play is playing,
And 'scape detecting, I will pay the theft.   80

> *Enter Trumpets and Kettledrums,* KING, QUEEN, POLONIUS,
> OPHELIA [ROSENCRANTZ, GUILDENSTERN, *and other* LORDS *at-*
> *tendant*].

HAM.   They are coming to the play. I must be idle.
Get you a place.
KING.   How fares our cousin Hamlet?
HAM.   Excellent, i' faith, of the chameleon's dish. I eat the air,
promise-crammed. You cannot feed capons so.   85
KING.   I have nothing with this answer, Hamlet. These words are not
mine.
HAM.   No, nor mine now. [*To* POLONIUS.] My lord, you played once
i' th' university, you say?
POL.   That did I, my lord, and was accounted a good actor.   90
HAM.   What did you enact?
POL.   I did enact Julius Cæsar. I was killed i' th' Capitol; Brutus
killed me.
HAM.   It was a brute part of him to kill so capital a calf there. Be the
players ready?   95
ROS.   Ay, my lord, they stay upon your patience.
QUEEN.   Come hither, my dear Hamlet, sit by me.

---

60. *comeddled* mingled.
70. *the very comment of thy soul* with a keenness
of observation that penetrates to the very being.
71. *occulted* hidden.
72. *unkennel* reveal.

75. *stithy* forge.
78. *censure* opinion.
81. *idle* crazy.
84. *chameleon's dish* the air, on which the chameleon was supposed to feed.

HAM.   No, good mother, here's metal more attractive.
POL.   [*To the* KING.] O, ho! do you mark that?
HAM.   Lady, shall I lie in your lap?   100

                    [*Lying down at* OPHELIA'S *feet.*]
OPH.   No, my lord.
HAM.   I mean, my head upon your lap?
OPH.   Ay, my lord.
HAM.   Do you think I meant country matters?
OPH.   I think nothing, my lord.   105
HAM.   That's a fair thought to lie between maids' legs.
OPH.   What is, my lord?
HAM.   Nothing.
OPH.   You are merry, my lord.
HAM.   Who, I?   110
OPH.   Ay, my lord.
HAM.   O God, your only jig-maker! What should a man do but be
   merry? For look you how cheerfully my mother looks, and my
   father died within's two hours.
OPH.   Nay, 'tis twice two months, my lord.   115
HAM.   So long? Nay then, let the devil wear black, for I'll have a
   suit of sables. O heavens! die two months ago, and not forgotten
   yet? Then there's hope a great man's memory may outlive his life
   half a year, but by'r lady 'a must build churches then, or else shall
   'a suffer not thinking on, with the hobby-horse, whose epitaph is 120
'For O, for O, the hobby-horse is forgot!'

                 The trumpets sound. Dumb Show follows.
Enter a KING *and a* QUEEN [*very lovingly*]; *the* QUEEN *embracing him
and he her.* [*She kneels, and makes show of protestation unto him.*]
*He takes her up, and declines his head upon her neck. He lies him
down upon a bank of flowers; she, seeing him asleep, leaves him.
Anon come in another man, takes off his crown, kisses it, pours
poison in the sleeper's ears, and leaves him. The* QUEEN *returns,
finds the* KING *dead, makes passionate action. The* POISONER *with
some three or four come in again, seem to condole with her. The
dead body is carried away. The* POISONER *woos the* QUEEN *with gifts;
she seems harsh awhile, but in the end accepts love.*   [*Exeunt.*]
OPH.   What means this, my lord?
HAM.   Marry, this is miching mallecho; it means mischief.
OPH.   Belike this show imports the argument of the play.

            Enter PROLOGUE.
HAM.   We shall know by this fellow. The players cannot keep coun- 125
sel; they'll tell all.
OPH.   Will 'a tell us what this show meant?

---

120. *hobby-horse* the figure of a horse fastened
round the waist of a morris dancer. Puritan efforts
to suppress the country sports in which the hobby-
horse figured led to a popular ballad lamenting the
fact that "the hobby-horse is forgot."
123. *miching mallecho* skulking or crafty crime.

HAM.   Ay, or any show that you will show him. Be not you ashamed
to show, he'll not shame to tell you what it means.

OPH.   You are naught, you are naught. I'll mark the play.   130

PRO.
>   For us, and for our tragedy,
>   Here stooping to your clemency,
>   We beg your hearing patiently.   [*Exit.*]

HAM.   Is this a prologue, or the posy of a ring?

OPH.   'Tis brief, my lord.   135

HAM.   As woman's love.

Enter [the PLAYER] KING *and* QUEEN.

P. KING.   *Full thirty times hath Phœbus' cart gone round*
>   *Neptune's salt wash and Tellus' orbéd ground,*
>   *And thirty dozen moons with borrowed sheen*
>   *About the world have times twelve thirties been,*   140
>   *Since love our hearts and Hymen did our hands*
>   *Unite comutual in most sacred bands.*

P. QUEEN.   *So many journeys may the sun and moon*
>   *Make us again count o'er ere love be done!*
>   *But woe is me, you are so sick of late,*   145
>   So far from cheer and from your former state,
>   *That I distrust you. Yet though I distrust,*
>   *Discomfort you, my lord, it nothing must.*
>   *For women's fear and love hold quantity,*
>   *In neither aught, or in extremity.*   150
>   *Now what my love is proof hath made you know,*
>   *And as my love is sized, my fear is so.*
>   *Where love is great, the littlest doubts are fear;*
>   *Where little fears grow great, great love grows there.*

P. KING.   *Faith, I must leave thee, love, and shortly too;*   155
>   *My operant powers their functions leave to do.*
>   *And thou shalt live in this fair world behind,*
>   *Honored, beloved, and haply one as kind*
>   *For husband shalt thou—*

P. QUEEN.   *O, confound the rest!*
>   *Such love must needs be treason in my breast.*   160
>   *In second husband let me be accurst!*
>   *None wed the second but who killed the first.*

HAM.   That's wormwood.

P. QUEEN.   *The instances that second marriage move*
>   *Are base respects of thrift, but none of love.*   165

---

130. *naught* naughty, lewd.
134. *posy* brief motto engraved on a finger-ring.
137. *Phœbus' cart* the sun's chariot.
138. *Tellus' orbed ground* the earth (Tellus was the Roman goddess of the earth).
141. *Hymen* god of marriage.

147. *distrust* fear for.
149. *hold quantity* are proportional, weigh alike.
152. *as my love is sized* according to the greatness of my love.
156. *operant* vital.
164. *instances* motives.

A second time I kill my husband dead,
When second husband kisses me in bed.
P. KING.   I do believe you think what now you speak,
But what we do determine oft we break.
Purpose is but the slave to memory,   170
Of violent birth, but poor validity;
Which now, the fruit unripe, sticks on the tree,
But fall unshaken when they mellow be.
Most necessary 'tis that we forget
To pay ourselves what to ourselves is debt.   175
What to ourselves in passion we propose,
The passion ending, doth the purpose lose.
The violence of either grief or joy
Their own enactures with themselves destroy.
Where joy most revels, grief doth most lament;   180
Grief joys, joy grieves, on slender accident.
This world is not for aye, nor 'tis not strange
That even our loves should with our fortunes change;
For 'tis a question left us yet to prove,
Whether love lead fortune, or else fortune love.   185
The great man down, you mark his favorite flies;
The poor advanced makes friends of enemies;
And hitherto doth love on fortune tend,
For who not needs shall never lack a friend,
And who in want a hollow friend doth try,   190
Directly seasons him his enemy.
But orderly to end where I begun,
Our wills and fates do so contrary run
That our devices still are overthrown;
Our thoughts are ours, their ends none of our own.   195
So think thou wilt no second husband wed,
But die thy thoughts when thy first lord is dead.
P. QUEEN.   Nor earth to me give food, nor heaven light,
Sport and repose lock from me day and night,
To desperation turn my trust and hope,   200
An anchor's cheer in prison be my scope,
Each opposite that blanks the face of joy
Meet what I would have well, and it destroy,
Both here and hence pursue me lasting strife,
If once a widow, ever I be wife!   205
HAM.   If she should break it now!
P. KING.   'Tis deeply sworn. Sweet, leave me here awhile.
My spirits grow dull, and fain I would beguile
The tedious day with sleep.   [Sleeps.]

171. *validity* endurance.   191. *seasons him* ripens him into.
179. *enactures* enactments.   201. *anchor's* anchorite's.
182. *aye* ever.

P. QUEEN   *Sleep rock thy brain,*
    And never come mischance between us twain!   *Exit.* 210
HAM.   Madam, how like you this play?
QUEEN.   The lady doth protest too much, methinks.
HAM.   O, but she'll keep her word.
KING.   Have you heard the argument? Is there no offence in't?
HAM.   No, no, they do but jest, poison in jest; no offence i' th' world. 215
KING.   What do you call the play?
HAM.   'The Mouse-trap.' Marry, how? Tropically. This play is the
    image of a murder done in Vienna. Gonzago is the duke's name;
    his wife, Baptista. You shall see anon. 'Tis a knavish piece of
    work, but what of that? Your majesty, and we that have free 220
    souls, it touches us not. Let the galled jade wince, our withers are
    unwrung.

        Enter LUCIANUS.
    This is one Lucianus, nephew to the king.
OPH.   You are as good as a chorus, my lord.
HAM.   I could interpret between you and your love, if I could see 225
    the puppets dallying.
OPH.   You are keen, my lord, you are keen.
HAM.   It would cost you a groaning to take off mine edge.
OPH.   Still better, and worse.
HAM.   So you mis-take your husbands.—Begin, murderer. Leave 230
    thy damnable faces and begin. Come, the croaking raven doth
    bellow for revenge.
LUC.   *Thoughts black, hands apt, drugs fit, and time agreeing,*
    Confederate season, else no creature seeing,
    Thou mixture rank, of midnight weeds collected,   235
    With Hecate's ban thrice blasted, thrice infected,
    Thy natural magic and dire property
    On wholesome life usurps immediately.
                        [*Pours the poison in his ears.*]
HAM.   'A poisons him i' th' garden for his estate. His name's Gon-
    zago. The story is extant, and written in very choice Italian. You 240
    shall see anon how the murderer gets the love of Gonzago's wife.
OPH.   The king rises.
HAM.   What, frighted with false fire?
QUEEN.   How fares my lord?
POL.   Give o'er the play.   245
KING.   Give me some light. Away!
POL.   Lights, lights, lights! *Exeunt all but* HAMLET *and* HORATIO.
HAM.   Why, let the strucken deer go weep,
                    The hart ungallèd play.

221. *gallad jade* sorebacked horse.   under a blight.
236. *Hecate* goddess of witchcraft; *blasted* fallen

For some must watch while some must sleep;   250
    Thus runs the world away.

Would not this, sir, and a forest of feathers—if the rest of my
fortunes turn Turk with me—with two Provincial roses on my razed
shoes, get me a fellowship in a cry of players?

HOR.   Half a share.   255

HAM.   A whole one, I.

    For thou dost know, O Damon dear,
        This realm dismantled was
    Of Jove himself, and now reigns here
        A very, very—pajock.   260

HOR.   You might have rhymed.

HAM.   O good Horatio, I'll take the ghost's word for a thousand pound.
Didst perceive?

HOR.   Very well, my lord.

HAM.   Upon the talk of the poisoning.   265

HOR.   I did very well note him.

HAM.   Ah, ha! Come, some music. Come, the recorders.

    For if the king like not the comedy,
    Why then, belike he likes it not, perdy.

Come, some music.   270

    Enter ROSENCRANTZ *and* GUILDENSTERN.

GUIL.   Good my lord, vouchsafe me a word with you.

HAM.   Sir, a whole history.

GUIL.   The king, sir—

HAM.   Ay, sir, what of him?

GUIL.   Is in his retirement marvellous distempered.   275

HAM.   With drink, sir?

GUIL.   No, my lord, with choler.

HAM.   Your wisdom should show itself more richer to signify this to
the doctor, for for me to put him to his purgation would perhaps
plunge him into more choler.   280

GUIL.   Good my lord, put your discourse into some frame, and start
not so wildly from my affair.

HAM.   I am tame, sir. Pronounce.

GUIL.   The queen your mother, in most great affliction of spirit,
hath sent me to you.   285

HAM.   You are welcome.

252. *feathers* plumes for actors' costumes.
253. *Provincial roses* i.e., Provençal roses. Ribbon rosettes resembling these French roses were used to decorate shoes; *razed* with ornamental slashing.
254. *cry* company.
260. *pajock* presumably a variant form of "patchcock," a despicable person. Cf. III.iv.104.

268. *For if . . . comedy* a seeming parody of *The Spanish Tragedy*, IV.i. 197–98 ("And if the world like not this tragedy,/Hard is the hap of old Hieronimo"), where another revenger's dramatic entertainment is referred to.
277. *choler* one of the four bodily humors, an excess of which gave rise to anger.

GUIL.   Nay, good my lord, this courtesy is not of the right breed. If
it shall please you to make me a wholesome answer, I will do your
mother's commandment. If not, your pardon and my return shall
be the end of my business.   290
HAM.   Sir, I cannot.
ROS.   What, my lord?
HAM.   Make you a wholesome answer; my wit's diseased. But, sir,
such answer as I can make, you shall command, or rather, as you
say, my mother. Therefore no more, but to the matter. My mother, 295
you say—
ROS.   Then thus she says: your behavior hath struck her into amaze-
ment and admiration.
HAM.   O wonderful son, that can so stonish a mother! But is there
no sequel at the heels of this mother's admiration? Impart.   300
ROS.   She desires to speak with you in her closet ere you go to bed.
HAM.   We shall obey, were she ten times our mother. Have you any
further trade with us?
ROS.   My lord, you once did love me.
HAM.   And do still, by these pickers and stealers.   305
ROS.   Good my lord, what is your cause of distemper? You do surely
bar the door upon your own liberty, if you deny your griefs to your
friend.
HAM.   Sir, I lack advancement.
ROS.   How can that be, when you have the voice of the king himself 310
for your succession in Denmark?
HAM.   Ay, sir, but 'while the grass grows'—the proverb is something
musty.

           Enter the PLAYERS *with recorders.*
O, the recorders! Let me see one. To withdraw with you—why do
you go about to recover the wind of me, as if you would drive me 315
into a toil?
GUIL.   O my lord, if my duty be too bold, my love is too unman-
nerly.
HAM.   I do not well understand that. Will you play upon this
pipe?   320
GUIL.   My lord, I cannot.
HAM.   I pray you.
GUIL.   Believe me, I cannot.
HAM.   I do beseech you.
GUIL.   I know no touch of it, my lord.   325
HAM.   It is as easy as lying. Govern these ventages with your fingers
and thumb, give it breath with your mouth, and it will discourse
most eloquent music. Look you, these are the stops.

288. *wholesome* reasonable.
300. *admiration* wonder.
305. *pickers and stealers* hands.
312. *"while the grass grows"* a proverb ending "the

horse starves."
314. *withdraw* step aside for private conversation.
316. *toil* net, snare.
326. *ventages* holes or stops in the recorder.

GUIL.　But these cannot I command to any utt'rance of harmony.
　　I have not the skill.   330
HAM.　Why, look you now, how unworthy a thing you make of
　　me! You would play upon me, you would seem to know my stops,
　　you would pluck out the heart of my mystery, you would sound
　　me from my lowest note to the top of my compass; and there is
　　　much music, excellent voice, in this little organ, yet cannot you 335
make it speak. 'Sblood, do you think I am easier to be played on than
　　a pipe? Call me what instrument you will, though you can fret
　　me, you cannot play upon me.

　　　　Enter POLONIUS.
　　God bless you, sir!
POL.　My lord, the queen would speak with you, and presently.   340
HAM.　Do you see yonder cloud that's almost in shape of a camel?
POL.　By th' mass and 'tis, like a camel indeed.
HAM.　Methinks it is like a weasel.
POL.　It is backed like a weasel.
HAM.　Or like a whale.   345
POL.　Very like a whale.
HAM.　Then I will come to my mother by and by. [*Aside.*] They fool
　　me to the top of my bent.—I will come by and by.
POL.　I will say so.   [*Exit* POLONIUS.]
HAM.　'By and by' is easily said. Leave me, friends.   350
　　　　　　　　　　　　　　　　　[*Exeunt all but* HAMLET.]
　　'Tis now the very witching time of night,
　　When churchyards yawn, and hell itself breathes out
　　Contagion to this world. Now could I drink hot blood,
　　And do such bitter business as the day
　　Would quake to look on. Soft, now to my mother.   355
　　O heart, lose not thy nature; let not ever
　　The soul of Nero enter this firm bosom.
　　Let me be cruel, not unnatural;
　　I will speak daggers to her, but use none.
　　My tongue and soul in this be hypocrites: 360
　　How in my words somever she be shent,
　　To give them seals never my soul consent!   *Exit.*

[III.iii]

　　　　Enter KING, ROSENCRANTZ, *and* GUILDENSTERN.
KING.　I like him not, nor stands it safe with us
　　To let his madness range. Therefore prepare you.
　　I your commission will forthwith dispatch,

338. *fret* (1) a stop on the fingerboard of a guitar
(2) annoy.
357. *Nero* Roman emperor who murdered his
mother.
361. *somever* soever; *shent* reproved, abused.

And he to England shall along with you.
The terms of our estate may not endure   5
Hazard so near's as doth hourly grow
Out of his brows.
GUIL.   We will ourselves provide,
Most holy and religious fear it is
To keep those many many bodies safe
That live and feed upon your majesty.   10
ROS.   The single and peculiar life is bound
With all the strength and armor of the mind
To keep itself from noyance, but much more
That spirit upon whose weal depends and rests
The lives of many. The cess of majesty   15
Dies not alone, but like a gulf doth draw
What's near it with it. It is a massy wheel
Fixed on the summit of the highest mount,
To whose huge spokes ten thousand lesser things
Are mortised and adjoined, which when it falls,   20
Each small annexment, petty consequence,
Attends the boist'rous ruin. Never alone
Did the king sigh, but with a general groan.
KING.   Arm you, I pray you, to this speedy voyage,
For we will fetters put about this fear,   25
Which now goes too free-footed.
ROS.   We will haste us.
                                             Exeunt Gentlemen.

        Enter POLONIUS.
POL.   My lord, he's going to his mother's closet.
Behind the arras I'll convey myself
To hear the process. I'll warrant she'll tax him home,
And as you said, and wisely was it said,   30
'Tis meet that some more audience than a mother,
Since nature makes them partial, should o'erhear
The speech of vantage. Fare you well, my liege.
I'll call upon you ere you go to bed,
And tell you what I know.
KING.   Thanks, dear my lord. *Exit* [POLONIUS]. 35
O, my offence is rank, it smells to heaven;
It hath the primal eldest curse upon't,
A brother's murder. Pray can I not,
Though inclination be as sharp as will.
My stronger guilt defeats my strong intent,   40

[III.iii] 5. *terms of our estate* conditions required
for our rule as king.
7. *brows* threatning looks that suggest the dangerous plots Hamlet's brain is hatching.
11. *peculiar* private.
13. *noyance* harm.

15. *cess* cessation, extinction.
20. *mortised* jointed (as with mortise and tenon).
33. *of vantage* (1) in addition; (2) from a convenient place for listening.
39. *will* carnal desire.

And like a man to double business bound,
I stand in pause where I shall first begin,
And both neglect. What if this cursèd hand
Were thicker than itself with brother's blood,
Is there not rain enough in the sweet heavens   45
To wash it white as snow? Whereto serves mercy
But to confront the visage of offence?
And what's in prayer but this twofold force,
To be forestallèd ere we come to fall,
Or pardoned being down? Then I'll look up.   50
My fault is past. But, O, what form of prayer
Can serve my turn? 'Forgive me my foul murder'?
That cannot be, since I am still possessed
Of those effects for which I did the murder—
My crown, mine own ambition, and my queen.   55
May one be pardoned and retain th' offence?
In the corrupted currents of this world
Offence's gilded hand may shove by justice,
And oft 'tis seen the wicked prize itself
Buys out the law. But 'tis not so above.   60
There is no shuffling; there the action lies
In his true nature, and we ourselves compelled,
Even to the teeth and forehead of our faults,
To give in evidence. What then? What rests?
Try what repentance can. What can it not?   65
Yet what can it when one can not repent?
O wretched state! O bosom black as death!
O limèd soul, that struggling to be free
Art more engaged! Help, angels! Make assay.
Bow, stubborn knees, and heart with strings of steel,   70
Be soft as sinews of the new-born babe.
All may be well.   [*He kneels.*]

        Enter HAMLET.
HAM.   Now might I do it pat, now 'a is a-praying,
        And now I'll do't—and so 'a goes to heaven,
        And so am I revenged. That would be scanned.   75
        A villain kills my father, and for that,
        I, his sole son, do this same villain send
        To heaven.
        Why, this is hire and salary, not revenge.
        'A took my father grossly, full of bread,   80
        With all his crimes broad blown, as flush as May;
        And how his audit stands who knows save heaven?

---

61. *shuffling* doubledealing; *action* legal action.   80. *grossly* unprepared spiritually.
68. *limed soul* caught by sin as the bird by lime.   81. *as flush as May* in full flower.
69. *assay* an effort.

But in our circumstance and course of thought
'Tis heavy with him; and am I then revenged
To take him in the purging of his soul,   85
When he is fit and seasoned for his passage?
No.
Up, sword, and know thou a more horrid hent.
When he is drunk asleep, or in his rage,
Or in th' incestuous pleasure of his bed,   90
At game a-swearing, or about some act
That has no relish of salvation in't—
Then trip him, that his heels may kick at heaven,
And that his soul may be as damned and black
As hell, whereto it goes. My mother stays.   95
This physic but prolongs thy sickly days.   *Exit.*
KING.   [*Rising.*] My words fly up, my thoughts remain below.
Words without thoughts never to heaven go.   *Exit.*

[III.iv]

Enter [QUEEN] GERTRUDE *and* POLONIUS.
POL.   'A will come straight. Look you lay home to him.
Tell him his pranks have been too broad to bear with,
And that your grace hath screen'd and stood between
Much heat and him. I'll silence me even here.
Pray you be round.
QUEEN.   I'll warrant you. Fear me not.   5
Withdraw, I hear him coming.
                              [POLONIUS *goes behind the arras.*]

Enter HAMLET.
HAM.   Now, mother, what's the matter?
QUEEN.   Hamlet, thou hast thy father much offended.
HAM.   Mother, you have my father much offended.
QUEEN.   Come, come, you answer with an idle tongue.   10
HAM.   Go, go, you question with a wicked tongue.
QUEEN.   Why, how now, Hamlet?
HAM.   What's the matter now?
QUEEN.   Have you forgot me?
HAM.   No, by the rood, not so.
You are the queen, your husband's brother's wife,
And would it were not so, you are my mother.   15

---

83.   *in our circumstance* considering all evidence; *course* beaten way, habit.
88.   *hent* occasion, opportunity.

[III.iv] 5.   Following Polonius's "Pray you be round" (which in F reads "Pray you be round with him"), F adds the line: "*Ham. within.* Mother, mother, mother." Of which Professor Jenkins remarks (SB,

13.35), "What sort of prince is this who cannot come to his mother's chamber without announcing his arrival by calling 'Mother' three times in the corridor?" A similar instance where the F text supplies offstage calls in support of onstage references to a character's approach occurs at IV.ii.1.
13.   *rood* cross.

QUEEN.   Nay, then I'll set those to you that can speak.
HAM.   Come, come, and sit you down. You shall not budge.
  You go not till I set you up a glass
  Where you may see the inmost part of you.
QUEEN.   What wilt thou do? Thou wilt not murder me?   20
  Help, ho!
POL.   [Behind.] What, ho! help!
HAM.   [Draws.] How now, a rat?
  Dead for a ducat, dead!
          [Thrusts his sword through the arras and kills POLONIUS.]
POL.   [Behind.] O, I am slain!   25
QUEEN.   O me, what hast thou done?
HAM.   Nay, I know not.
  Is it the king?
QUEEN.   O, what a rash and bloody deed is this!
HAM.   A bloody deed? Almost as bad, good mother,
  As kill a king and marry with his brother.   30
QUEEN.   As kill a king?
HAM.   Ay, lady, it was my word.
          [Lifts up the arras and sees the body of POLONIUS.]
  Thou wretched, rash, intruding fool, farewell!
  I took thee for thy better. Take thy fortune.
  Thou find'st to be too busy is some danger.—
  Leave wringing of your hands. Peace, sit you down   35
  And let me wring your heart, for so I shall
  If it be made of penetrable stuff,
  If damnéd custom have not brazed it so
  That it be proof and bulwark against sense.
QUEEN.   What have I done that thou dar'st wag thy tongue   40
  In noise so rude against me?
HAM.   Such an act
  That blurs the grace and blush of modesty,
  Calls virtue hypocrite, takes off the rose
  From the fair forehead of an innocent love,
  And sets a blister there, makes marriage-vows   45
  As false as dicers' oaths. O, such a deed
  As from the body of contraction plucks
  The very soul, and sweet religion makes
  A rhapsody of words. Heaven's face does glow
  O'er this solidity and compound mass   50
  With heated visage, as against the doom—
  Is thought-sick at the act.
QUEEN.   Ay me, what act,

---

38. *brazed* plated it as with brass.
39. *proof* impenetrable, as of armor.
47. *contraction* the contract of marriage.

50. *this solidity and compound mass* the earth, as
compounded of the four elements.
51. *doom* Judgment Day.

That roars so loud and thunders in the index?
HAM.   Look here upon this picture and on this,
The counterfeit presentment of two brothers.   55
See what a grace was seated on this brow:
Hyperion's curls, the front of Jove himself,
An eye like Mars, to threaten and command,
A station like the herald Mercury
New lighted on a heaven-kissing hill—   60
A combination and a form indeed
Where every god did seem to set his seal
To give the world assurance of a man.
This was your husband. Look you now what follows.
Here is your husband, like a mildewed ear   65
Blasting his wholesome brother. Have you eyes?
Could you on this fair mountain leave to feed,
And batten on this moor? Ha, have you eyes?
You cannot call it love, for at your age
The heyday in the blood is tame, it's humble,   70
And waits upon the judgment, and what judgment
Would step from this to this? Sense sure you have,
Else could you not have motion, but sure that sense
Is apoplexed, for madness would not err
Nor sense to ecstasy was ne'er so thralled   75
But it reserved some quantity of choice
To serve in such a difference. What devil was't
That thus hath cozened you at hoodman-blind?
Eyes without feeling, feeling without sight,
Ears without hands or eyes, smelling sans all,   80
Or but a sickly part of one true sense
Could not so mope. O shame, where is thy blush?
Rebellious hell,
If thou canst mutine in a matron's bones,
To flaming youth let virtue be as wax   85
And melt in her own fire. Proclaim no shame
When the compulsive ardor gives the charge,
Since frost itself as actively doth burn,
And reason panders will.
QUEEN.   O Hamlet, speak no more!
Thou turn'st my eyes into my very soul,   90

53. *index* table of contents; thus, indication of what
is to follow.
55. *counterfeit presentment* portrait.
57. *front* forehead.
59. *station* bearing, figure.
68. *batten* feed like an animal.
70. *heyday* ardor.
72. *Sense* the senses collectively, which according
to Aristotelian tradition are found in all creatures
that have the power of locomotion.
75. *ecstasy* madness.
78. *hoodman-blind* blindman's bluff.
80. *sans* without.
82. *mope* act without full use of one's wits.
89. *will* desire.

And there I see such black and grainéd spots
As will not leave their tinct.
HAM.   Nay, but to live
  In the rank sweat of an enseaméd bed,
  Stewed in curruption, honeying and making love
  Over the nasty sty—
QUEEN.   O, speak to me no more!   95
  These words like daggers enter in my ears.
  No more, sweet Hamlet.
HAM.   A murderer and a villain,
  A slave that is not twentieth part the tithe
  Of your precedent lord, a vice of kings,
  A cutpurse of the empire and the rule,   100
  That from a shelf the precious diadem stole
  And put it in his pocket—
QUEEN.   No more.

          Enter GHOST.
HAM.   A king of shreds and patches—
  Save me and hover o'er me with your wings,   105
  You heavenly guards! What would your gracious figure?
QUEEN.   Alas, he's mad.
HAM.   Do you not come your tardy son to chide,
  That lapsed in time and passion lets go by
  Th' important acting of your dread command?   110
  O, say!
GHOST.   Do not forget. This visitation
  Is but to whet thy almost blunted purpose.
  But look, amazement on thy mother sits.
  O, step between her and her fighting soul!   115
  Conceit in weakest bodies strongest works.
  Speak to her, Hamlet.
HAM.   How is it with you, lady?
QUEEN.   Alas, how is't with you,
  That you do bend your eye on vacancy,
  And with th' incorporal air do hold discourse?   120
  Forth at your eyes your spirits wildly peep,
  And as the sleeping soldiers in th' alarm,
  Your bedded hair like life in excrements
  Start up and stand an end. O gentle son,
  Upon the heat and flame of thy distemper   125
  Sprinkle cool patience. Whereon do you look?

91. *grainéd spots* indelible stains.
92. *tinct* color.
93. *enseamed* greasy.
99. *vice* a character in the morality plays, presented often as a buffoon (here, a caricature).

116. *Conceit* imagination.
123. *excrements* nails, hair (whatever grows out of the body).
124. *an* on.

HAM.   On him, on him! Look you how pale he glares.
  His form and cause conjoined, preaching to stones,
  Would make them capable.—Do not look upon me,
  Lest with this piteous action you convert   130
  My stern effects. Then what I have to do
  Will want true color—tears perchance for blood.
QUEEN.   To whom do you speak this?
HAM.   Do you see nothing there?
QUEEN.   Nothing at all, yet all that is I see.   135
HAM.   Nor did you nothing hear?
QUEEN.   No, nothing but ourselves.
HAM.   Why, look you there. Look how it steals away.
  My father, in his habit as he lived!
  Look where he goes even now out at the portal.   *Exit* GHOST. 140
QUEEN.   This is the very coinage of your brain.
  This bodiless creation ecstasy
  Is very cunning in.
HAM.   My pulse as yours doth temperately keep time,
  And makes as healthful music. It is not madness   145
  That I have uttered. Bring me to the test,
  And I the matter will re-word, which madness
  Would gambol from. Mother, for love of grace,
  Lay not that flattering unction to your soul,
  That not your trespass but my madness speaks.   150
  It will but skin and film the ulcerous place
  Whiles rank corruption, mining all within,
  Infects unseen. Confess yourself to heaven,
  Repent what's past, avoid what is to come,
  And do not spread the compost on the weeds,   155
  To make them ranker. Forgive me this my virtue,
  For in the fatness of these pursy times
  Virtue itself of vice must pardon beg,
  Yea, curb and woo for leave to do him good.
QUEEN.   O Hamlet, thou hast cleft my heart in twain.   160
HAM.   O, throw away the worser part of it,
  And live the purer with the other half.
  Good night—but go not to my uncle's bed.
  Assume a virtue, if you have it not.
  That monster custom, who all sense doth eat,   165
  Of habits devil, is angel yet in this,

---

129. *capable* able to respond.
132. *want* lack.
148. *gambol* leap or start, as a shying horse.
149. *unction* ointment; hence, soothing notion.
152. *mining* undermining.
157. *fatness* grossness, slackness; *pursy* corpulent.
165. *who all sense doth eat* who consumes all human sense, both bodily and spiritual.

166. *Of habits devil* being a devil in, or in respect of, habits (with a play on "habits," as meaning both settled practices and garments, whereby devilish practices contrast with "actions fair and good," line 167, and devilish garments contrast with the "frock or livery" of line 168, which custom in its angelic aspect provides).

That to the use of actions fair and good
He likewise gives a frock or livery
That aptly is put on. Refrain to-night,
And that shall lend a kind of easiness   170
To the next abstinence; the next more easy;
For use almost can change the stamp of nature,
And either curb the devil, or throw him out
With wondrous potency. Once more, good night,
And when you are desirous to be blest,   175
I'll blessing beg of you. For this same lord
I do repent; but heaven hath pleased it so,
To punish me with this, and this with me,
That I must be their scourge and minister.
I will bestow him and will answer well   180
The death I gave him. So, again, good night.
I must be cruel only to be kind.
This bad begins and worse remains behind.
One word more, good lady.
QUEEN.   What shall I do?
HAM.   Not this, by no means, that I bid you do: 185
Let the bloat king tempt you again to bed,
Pinch wanton on your cheek, call you his mouse,
And let him, for a pair of reechy kisses,
Or paddling in your neck with his damned fingers,
Make you to ravel all this matter out,   190
That I essentially am not in madness,
But mad in craft. 'Twere good you let him know,
For who that's but a queen, fair, sober, wise,
Would from a paddock, from a bat, a gib,
Such dear concernings hide? Who would so do?   195
No, in despite of sense and secrecy,
Unpeg the basket on the house's top,
Let the birds fly, and like the famous ape,
To try conclusions, in the basket creep
And break your own neck down.   200
QUEEN.   Be thou assured, if words be made of breath
And breath of life, I have no life to breathe
What thou hast said to me.
HAM.   I must to England; you know that?
QUEEN.   Alack,
I had forgot. 'Tis so concluded on.   205

183. *This* i.e., the death of Polonius (cf. line 178); *remains behind* is yet to come.
188. *reechy* dirty.
191. *essentially* in fact.
194. *paddock* toad; *gib* tom-cat.
197–200. *Unpeg the basket* * * * *neck down* the story is lost (in it, apparently, the ape carries a cage of birds to the top of a house, releases them by accident, and, surprised at their flight, imagines he can imitate it by first creeping into the basket and then leaping out. The moral of the story, for the queen, is not to expose herself to destruction by making public what good sense decrees should be kept secret.).

HAM.   There's letters sealed, and my two school-fellows,
        Whom I will trust as I will adders fanged,
        They bear the mandate; they must sweep my way
        And marshal me to knavery. Let it work,
        For 'tis the sport to have the engineer   210
        Hoist with his own petar; and't shall go hard
        But I will delve one yard below their mines
        And blow them at the moon. O, 'tis most sweet
        When in one line two crafts directly meet.
        This man shall set me packing.   215
        I'll lug the guts into the neighbour room.
        Mother, good night indeed. This counsellor
        Is now most still, most secret, and most grave,
        Who was in life a foolish prating knave.
        Come sir, to draw toward an end with you.   220
        Good night, mother.

                          Exit [HAMLET *tugging in* POLONIUS].

[IV.i]

         Enter KING [TO THE] QUEEN, *with* ROSENCRANTZ *and* GUIL-
         DENSTERN.

KING.   There's matter in these sighs, these profound heaves,
         You must translate; 'tis fit we understand them.
         Where is your son?
QUEEN.   Bestow this place on us a little while.
                          [*Exeunt* ROSENCRANTZ *and* GUILDENSTERN.]
         Ah, mine own lord, what have I seen to-night!   5
KING.   What, Gertrude, how does Hamlet?
QUEEN.   Mad as the sea and wind when both contend
         Which is the mightier. In his lawless fit,
         Behind the arras hearing something stir,
         Whips out his rapier, cries 'A rat, a rat!'   10
         And in this brainish apprehension kills
         The unseen good old man.
KING.   O heavy deed!
         It had been so with us had we been there.
         His liberty is full of threats to all—
         To your yourself, to us, to every one.   15
         Alas, how shall this bloody deed be answered?
         It will be laid to us, whose providence
         Should have kept short, restrained, and out of haunt,
         This mad young man. But so much was our love,

---

211. *petar* a bomb or charge for blowing in gates.
217. *indeed* in earnest (cf. lines 163, 174, 181)

[IV.i] The action is continuous with that of the
preceding scene. The Queen does not leave the
stage. Concerning the traditional editorial division

of Acts III and IV, see Granville-Barker, below,
pp. 192–93, 194–95.
2. *translate* explain.
11. *brainish apprehension* frenzied delusion.
18. *out of haunt* away from society.

We would not understand what was most fit,   20
But like the owner of a foul disease,
To keep it from divulging, let it feed
Even on the pith of life. Where is he gone?
QUEEN.   To draw apart the body he hath killed,
O'er whom his very madness, like some ore   25
Among a mineral of metals base,
Shows itself pure: 'a weeps for what is done.
KING.   O Gertrude, come away!
The sun no sooner shall the mountains touch
But we will ship him hence, and this vile deed   30
We must with all our majesty and skill
Both countenance and excuse. Ho, Guildenstern!

     Enter ROSENCRANTZ *and* GUILDENSTERN.
Friends both, go join you with some further aid.
Hamlet in madness hath Polonius slain,
And from his mother's closet hath he dragged him.   35
Go seek him out; speak fair, and bring the body
Into the chapel. I pray you haste in this.
     [*Exeunt* ROSENCRANTZ *and* GUILDENSTERN.]
Come, Gertrude, we'll call up our wisest friends
And let them know both what we mean to do
And what's untimely done; so haply slander—   40
Whose whisper o'er the world's diameter,
As level as the cannon to his blank,
Transports his poisoned shot—may miss our name,
And hit the woundless air. O, come away!
My soul is full of discord and dismay.   *Exeunt.* 45

[IV.ii]

     Enter HAMLET.
HAM.   Safely stowed.—But soft, what noise? Who calls on Hamlet?
O, here they come.

     [*Enter*] ROSENCRANTZ, [GUILDENSTERN,] *and* OTHERS.
ROS.   What have you done, my lord, with the dead body?
HAM.   Compounded it with dust, whereto 'tis kin.
ROS.   Tell us where 'tis, that we may take it thence   5
And bear it to the chapel.
HAM.   Do not believe it.
ROS.   Believe what?
HAM.   That I can keep your counsel and not mine own. Besides,

---

26. *mineral* mine.
42. *As level* as sure of aim; *blank* target.

[IV.ii] 1. After the words "Safely stowed," F adds
the line: "*Gentlemen within. Hamlet, Lord Ham-*

let." Here, as at III.iv.5, "when a character speaks
of hearing someone coming, F provides, though
Q does not, for the audience to hear it too" (Jenkins, *SB*, 13.35).

to be demanded of a sponge—what replication should be made by 10
the son of a king?

ROS.   Take you me for a sponge, my lord?

HAM.   Ay, sir, that soaks up the king's countenance, his rewards,
his authorities. But such officers do the king best service in the
end. He keeps them like an apple in the corner of his jaw, first 15
mouthed to be last swallowed. When he needs what you have
gleaned, it is but squeezing you and, sponge, you shall be dry
again.

ROS.   I understand you not, my lord.

HAM.   I am glad of it. A knavish speech sleeps in a foolish ear.   20

ROS.   My lord, you must tell us where the body is, and go with us
to the king.

HAM.   The body is with the king, but the king is not with the body.
The king is a thing—

GUIL.   A thing, my lord!   25

HAM.   Of nothing. Bring me to him. Hide fox, and all after.

Exeunt.

[IV.iii]

Enter KING, *and two or three.*

KING.   I have sent to seek him, and to find the body.
How dangerous is it that this man goes loose!
Yet must not we put the strong law on him.
He's loved of the distracted multitude,
Who like not in their judgment but their eyes,   5
And where 'tis so, th' offender's scourge is weighed,
But never the offence. To bear all smooth and even,
This sudden sending him away must seem
Deliberate pause. Diseases desperate grown
By desperate appliance are relieved,   10
Or not at all.

Enter ROSENCRANTZ, [GUILDENSTERN,] *and all the rest.*
How now! what hath befall'n?

ROS.   Where the dead body is bestowed, my lord,
We cannot get from him.

KING.   But where is he?

ROS.   Without, my lord; guarded, to know your pleasure.

KING.   Bring him before us.

ROS.   Ho! bring in the lord.   15

They enter [with HAMLET].

KING.   Now, Hamlet, where's Polonius?

---

10. *replication* reply.
26. *Hide fox, and all after* presumably a cry in
some game such as hide-and-seek. The words,
which do not occur in Q2, may be an actor's ad-

dition.

[IV.iii] 9. *Deliberate pause* carefully considered.

HAM.   At supper.

KING.   At supper? Where?

HAM.   Not where he eats, but where 'a is eaten. A certain convo-
cation of politic worms are e'en at him. Your worm is your only   20
emperor for diet. We fat all creatures else to fat us, and we fat
ourselves for maggots. Your fat king and your lean beggar is but
variable service—two dishes, but to one table. That's the end.

KING.   Alas, alas!

HAM.   A man may fish with the worm that hath eat of a king, and   25
eat of the fish that hath fed of that worm.

KING.   What dost thou mean by this?

HAM.   Nothing but to show you how a king may go a progress through
the guts of a beggar.

KING.   Where is Polonius?   30

HAM.   In heaven. Send thither to see. If your messenger find him
not there, seek him i' th' other place yourself. But if, indeed, you
find him not within this month, you shall nose him as you go up
the stairs into the lobby.

KING.   [To ATTENDANTS.] Go seek him there.   35

HAM.   'A will stay till you come.   [Exeunt ATTENDANTS.]

KING.   Hamlet, this deed, for thine especial safety—
Which we do tender, as we dearly grieve
For that which thou hast done—must send thee hence
With fiery quickness. Therefore prepare thyself.   40
The bark is ready, and the wind at help,
Th' associates tend, and everything is bent
For England.

HAM.   For England?

KING.   Ay, Hamlet.

HAM.   Good.

KING.   So is it, if thou knew'st our purposes.

HAM.   I see a cherub that sees them. But come, for England!   45
Farewell, dear mother.

KING.   Thy loving father, Hamlet.

HAM.   My mother. Father and mother is man and wife, man and
wife is one flesh. So, my mother. Come, for England.   Exit.

KING.   Follow him at foot; tempt him with speed aboard.   50
Delay it not; I'll have him hence to-night.
Away! for everything is sealed and done
That else leans on th' affair. Pray you make haste.
                              [Exeunt all but the KING.]
And, England, if my love thou hold'st at aught—
As my great power thereof may give thee sense,   55

---

28. *progress* the state journey of a ruler.
38. *tender* value.
45. *cherub* one of the cherubim, the watchmen or

sentinels of heaven, and thus endowed with the
keenest vision.

Since yet thy cicatrice looks raw and red
After the Danish sword, and thy free awe
Pays homage to us—thou mayst not coldly set
Our sovereign process, which imports at full
By letters congruing to that effect   60
The present death of Hamlet. Do it, England,
For like the hectic in my blood he rages,
And thou must cure me. Till I know 'tis done,
Howe'er my haps, my joys were ne'er begun.   *Exit.*

[IV.iv]

         Enter FORTINBRAS *with his* ARMY *over the stage.*
FORT.   Go, captain, from me greet the Danish king.
  Tell him that by his licence Fortinbras
  Craves the conveyance of a promised march
  Over his kingdom. You know the rendezvous.
  If that his majesty would aught with us,   5
  We shall express our duty in his eye,
  And let him know so.
CAP.   I will do't, my lord.
FORT.   Go softly on.   [*Exeunt all but the* CAPTAIN.]

        Enter HAMLET, ROSENCRANTZ, [GUILDENSTERN,] *and* OTHERS.
HAM.   Good sir, whose powers are these?
CAP.   They are of Norway, sir.   10
HAM.   How purposed, sir, I pray you?
CAP.   Against some part of Poland.
HAM.   Who commands them, sir?
CAP.   The nephew to old Norway, Fortinbras.
HAM.   Goes it against the main of Poland, sir,   15
  Or for some frontier?
CAP.   Truly to speak, and with no addition,
  We go to gain a little patch of ground
  That hath in it no profit but the name.
  To pay five ducats, five, I would not farm it;   20
  Nor will it yield to Norway or the Pole
  A ranker rate should it be sold in fee.
HAM.   Why, then the Polack never will defend it.
CAP.   Yes, it is already garrisoned.
HAM.   Two thousand souls and twenty thousand ducats   25

56. *cicatrice* scar, used here of memory of a defeat.
58. *coldly set* regard with indifference.
59. *process* mandate.
60. *congruing to* in accordance with.
62. *hectic* consumptive fever.
64. *haps* fortunes.

[IV.iv] 3. *conveyance* conduct.
6. *eye* presence.
15. *main* chief part.
17. *addition* exaggeration.
20. To *pay* i.e., for a yearly rental.
22. *a ranker rate* a greater price; *sold in fee* sold
with absolute and perpetual possession.

Will not debate the question of this straw.
This is th' imposthume of much wealth and peace,
That inward breaks, and shows no cause without
Why the man dies. I humbly thank you, sir.
CAP.   God buy you, sir.   [*Exit.*]
ROS.   Will't please you go, my lord?   30
HAM.   I'll be with you straight. Go a little before.
                                    [*Exeunt all but* HAMLET.]
How all occasions do inform against me,
And spur my dull revenge! What is a man,
If his chief good and market of his time
Be but to sleep and feed? A beast, no more.   35
Sure he that made us with such large discourse,
Looking before and after, gave us not
That capability and godlike reason
To fust in us unused. Now, whether it be
Bestial oblivion, or some craven scruple   40
Of thinking too precisely on th' event—
A thought which, quartered, hath but one part wisdom
And ever three parts coward—I do not know
Why yet I live to say 'This thing's to do',
Sith I have cause, and will, and strength, and means, 45
To do't. Examples gross as earth exhort me:
Witness this army of such mass and charge,
Led by a delicate and tender prince,
Whose spirit, with divine ambition puffed,
Makes mouths at the invisible event,   50
Exposing what is mortal and unsure
To all that fortune, death, and danger dare,
Even for an eggshell. Rightly to be great
Is not to stir without great argument,
But greatly to find quarrel in a straw   55
When honor's at the stake. How stand I then,
That have a father killed, a mother stained,
Excitements of my reason and my blood,
And let all sleep, while to my shame I see
The imminent death of twenty thousand men   60
That for a fantasy and trick of fame
Go to their graves like beds, fight for a plot
Whereon the numbers cannot try the cause,

27. *imposthume* abscess.
32. *inform* take shape.
34. *market* profit.
36. *discourse* power of reasoning.
39. *fust* grow musty.
50. *Makes mouths at* makes scornful faces at,
derides.

53–56. *Rightly to be great . . . honor's at the stake*
i.e., to be rightly great is *not* to refuse to act ("stir")
in a dispute ("argument") because the grounds are
insufficient, but to be moved to action even in trivial circumstances where a question of honor is in-
volved.
63. *try the cause* settle by combat.

Which is not tomb enough and continent
To hide the slain? O, from this time forth,   65
My thoughts be bloody, or be nothing worth!   *Exit.*

[IV.v]

      Enter HORATIO, [QUEEN] GERTRUDE, *and a* GENTLEMAN.
QUEEN.   I will not speak with her.
GENT.   She is importunate, indeed distract.
  Her mood will needs be pitied.
QUEEN.   What would she have?
GENT.   She speaks much of her father, says she hears
  There's tricks i' th' world, and hems, and beats her heart,   5
  Spurns enviously at straws, speaks things in doubt
  That carry but half sense. Her speech is nothing,
  Yet the unshaped use of it doth move
  The hearers to collection; they aim at it,
  And botch the words up fit to their own thoughts,   10
  Which, as her winks and nods and gestures yield them,
  Indeed would make one think there might be thought,
  Though nothing sure, yet much unhappily.
HOR.   'Twere good she were spoken with, for she may strew
  Dangerous conjectures in ill-breeding minds.   15
QUEEN.   Let her come in.   [*Exit* GENTLEMAN.]
  [*Aside.*] To my sick soul, as sin's true nature is,
  Each toy seems prologue to some great amiss.
  So full of artless jealousy is guilt,
  It spills itself in fearing to be spilt.   20

        Enter OPHELIA [*distracted*].
OPH.   Where is the beauteous majesty of Denmark?
QUEEN.   How now, Ophelia?
OPH.   How should I your true love know   *She sings.*
                From another one?
                By his cockle hat and staff,   25
                And his sandal shoon.
QUEEN.   Alas, sweet lady, what imports this song?
OPH.   Say you? Nay, pray you mark.

             He is dead and gone, lady,   (*Song.*)
             He is dead and gone;   30

---

64. *continent* receptacle.

[IV.v] 6. *Spurns enviously at straws* takes exception, spitefully, to trifles.
7. *nothing* nonsense.
8. *unshaped use* disordered manner.
9. *collection* attempts at shaping meaning; *aim*
guess.

13. *sure* certain.
18. *toy* trifle.
19. *artless jealousy* ill-concealed suspicion.
20. *spills* destroys.
25. *cockle hat* hat bearing a cockle shell, worn by
a pilgrim who had been to the shrine of St. James
of Compostella, in Spain.
26. *shoon* shoes.

                   At his head a grass-green turf,
                   At his heels a stone.

O, ho!
QUEEN: Nay, but Ophelia—
OPH.   Pray you mark.
         [*Sings.*] White his shroud as the mountain snow—   35

         Enter KING.
QUEEN.   Alas, look here, my lord.
OPH.   Larded all with sweet flowers;   (*Song.*)
                           Which bewept to the grave did not go
                           With true-love showers.
KING.   How do you, pretty lady?   40
OPH.   Well, good dild you! They say the owl was a baker's daughter.
   Lord, we know what we are, but know not what we may be. God
   be at your table!
KING.   Conceit upon her father.
OPH.   Pray let's have no words of this, but when they ask you what   45
   it means, say you this:

                   To-morrow is Saint Valentine's day,   (*Song.*)
                      All in the morning betime,
                   And I a maid at your window,
                      To be your Valentine.   50
                   Then up he rose, and donn'd his clo'es,
                      And dupped the chamber-door,
                   Let in the maid, that out a maid
                      Never departed more.
KING.   Pretty Ophelia—   55
OPH.   Indeed, without an oath, I'll make an end on't.

[*Sings.*]   By Gis and by Saint Charity,
                      Alack, and fie for shame!
                   Young men will do't, if they come to't;
                      By Cock, they are to blame.   60
                   Quoth she 'Before you tumbled me,
                      You promised me to wed'.

He answers:

                   'So would I 'a done, by yonder sun,
                   An thou hadst not come to my bed'.   65

---

37. *Larded* garnished, strewn.
41. *good dild you* God yield (requite) you.
41. *They say the owl was a baker's daughter* allusion to a folktale in which a baker's daughter was
transformed into an owl because of her ungener-
ous behavior (giving short measure) when Christ
asked for bread in the baker's shop.

44. *Conceit upon her father* i.e., obsessed with her
father's death.
48. *betime* early.
52. *dupped* opened.
57. *Gis* Jesus.
60. *Cock* corruption of God.

KING.   How long hath she been thus?
OPH.   I hope all will be well. We must be patient, but I cannot
    choose but weep to think they would lay him i' th' cold ground.
    My brother shall know of it, and so I thank you for your good
    counsel. Come, my coach! Good night, ladies, good night. Sweet   70
    ladies, good night, good night.   [Exit.]
KING.   Follow her close; give her good watch, I pray you.
                            [Exeunt HORATIO and GENTLEMAN.]
    O, this is the poison of deep grief; it springs
    All from her father's death, and now behold!
    O Gertrude, Gertrude!   75
    When sorrows come, they come not single spies,
    But in battalions: first, her father slain;
    Next, your son gone, and he most violent author
    Of his own just remove; the people muddied,
    Thick and unwholesome in their thoughts and whispers   80
    For good Polonius' death; and we have done but greenly
    In hugger-mugger to inter him; poor Ophelia
    Divided from herself and her fair judgment,
    Without the which we are pictures, or mere beasts;
    Last, and as much containing as all these,   85
    Her brother is in secret come from France,
    Feeds on his wonder, keeps himself in clouds,
    And wants not buzzers to infect his ear
    With pestilent speeches of his father's death,
    Wherein necessity, of matter beggared,   90
    Will nothing stick our person to arraign
    In ear and ear. O my dear Gertrude, this,
    Like to a murd'ring piece, in many places
    Gives me superfluous death. Attend,   A noise within.

        Enter a MESSENGER.
    Where are my Switzers? Let them guard the door.   95
    What is the matter?
MESS.   Save yourself, my lord.
    The ocean, overpeering of his list,
    Eats not the flats with more impiteous haste
    Then young Laertes, in a riotous head,
    O'erbears your officers. The rabble call him lord,   100
    And as the world were now but to begin,

79. *remove* banishment, departure; *muddied* stirred
up and confused.
81. *greenly* without judgment.
82. *hugger-mugger* secrecy and disorder.
87. *in clouds* i.e., of suspicion and rumor.
88. *wants* lacks.
90. *of matter beggared* lacking facts.
91. *nothing stick* in no way hesitate.
93. *murd'ring piece* cannon loaded with shot meant
to scatter.
94. *F* omits the King's "Attend," but substitutes,
by way of drawing attention to the "noise within,"
what Jenkins (*SB* 13.36) terms "a more obvious
exclamation from the Queen: 'Alacke, what noyse
is this?' "
95. *Switzers* Swiss bodyguard.
97. *list* boundary.
99. *riotous head* turbulent mob.

Antiquity forgot, custom not known,
The ratifiers and props of every word,
They cry 'Choose we, Laertes shall be king'.
Caps, hands, and tongues, applaud it to the clouds,   105
'Laertes shall be king, Laertes king'.
QUEEN.   How cheerfully on the false trail they cry!   *A noise within.*
O, this is counter, you false Danish dogs!
KING.   The doors are broke.

Enter LAERTES, *with* OTHERS.

LAER.   Where is this king?—Sirs, stand you all without.   110
ALL.   No, let's come in.
LAER.   I pray you give me leave.
ALL.   We will, we will.   [*Exeunt his followers.*]
LAER.   I thank you. Keep the door.—O thou vile king,
Give me my father!
QUEEN.   Calmly, good Laertes.
LAER.   That drop of blood that's calm proclaims me bastard,   115
Cries cuckold to my father, brands the harlot
Even here between the chaste unsmirchéd brow
Of my true mother.
KING.   What is the cause, Laertes,
That thy rebellion looks so giant-like?
Let him go, Gertrude. Do not fear our person.   120
There's such divinity doth hedge a king
That treason can but peep to what it would,
Acts little of his will. Tell me, Laertes.
Why thou art thus incensed. Let him go, Gertrude.
Speak, man.   125
LAER.   Where is my father?
KING.   Dead.
QUEEN.   But not by him.
KING.   Let him demand his fill.
LAER.   How came he dead? I'll not be juggled with.
To hell allegiance, vows to the blackest devil,
Conscience and grace to the profoundest pit!   130
I dare damnation. To this point I stand,
That both the worlds I give to negligence,
Let come what comes, only I'll be revenged
Most throughly for my father.
KING.   Who shall stay you?
LAER.   My will, not all the world's.   135
And for my means, I'll husband them so well
They shall go far with little.
KING.   Good Laertes,

108. *counter* hunting backward on the trail.   134. *throughly* thoroughly.
120. *fear* fear for.

If you desire to know the certainty
Of your dear father, is't writ in your revenge
That, swoopstake, you will draw both friend and foe,   140
Winner and loser?
LAER.   None but his enemies.
KING.   Will you know them, then?
LAER.   To his good friends thus wide I'll ope my arms,
And like the kind life-rend'ring pelican,
Repast them with my blood.
KING.   Why, now you speak   145
Like a good child and a true gentleman.
That I am guiltless of your father's death,
And am most sensibly in grief for it,
It shall as level to your judgment 'pear
As day does to your eye.
                              A *noise within:* 'Let her come in.' 150
LAER.   How now? What noise is that?

          Enter OPHELIA.
O, heat dry up my brains! tears seven times salt
Burn out the sense and virtue of mine eye!
By heaven, thy madness shall be paid with weight
Till our scale turn the beam. O rose of May,   155
Dear maid, kind sister, sweet Ophelia!
O heavens! is't possible a young maid's wits
Should be as mortal as an old man's life?
Nature is fine in love, and where 'tis fine
It sends some precious instance of itself   160
After the thing it loves.
OPH.   They bore him barefac'd on the bier;   (*Song.*)
               Hey non nonny, nonny, hey nonny;
               And in his grave rain'd many a tear—

Fare you well, my dove!   165
LAER.   Hadst thou thy wits, and didst persuade revenge,
It could not move thus.
OPH.   You must sing 'A-down, a-down,' and you 'Call him a-down-
a.' O, how the wheel becomes it! It is the false steward, that stole
his master's daughter.   170
LAER.   This nothing's more than matter.
OPH.   There's rosemary, that's for remembrance. Pray you, love, re-
member. And there is pansies, that's for thoughts.

---

140. *swoopstake* sweepstake, taking all the stakes
on the gambling table.
144. *pelican* supposed to feed her young with her
own blood.
149. *level* plain.

153. *virtue* power.
159. *fine* refined to purity.
169. *wheel* burden, refrain.
172–78. Harold Jenkins in his Arden edition of
Hamlet (London and New York, 1982) 536–42,

LAER. A document in madness, thoughts and remembrance fit-
ted.

OPH. There's fennel for you, and columbines. There's rue for you, 175
and here's some for me. We may call it herb of grace a Sundays.
O, you must wear your rue with a difference. There's a daisy. I
would give you some violets, but they withered all when my father
died. They say 'a made a good end.

[*Sings.*]   For bonny sweet Robin is all my joy.   180

LAER. Thought and affliction, passion, hell itself,
She turns to favor and to prettiness.

OPH.   And will 'a not come again?   (*Song.*)
                       And will 'a not come again?
                          No, no, he is dead,   185
                          Go to thy death-bed,
                       He never will come again.

                       His beard was as white as snow,
                       All flaxen was his poll;
                          He is gone, he is gone,   190
                          And we cast away moan:
                       God-a-mercy on his soul!

And of all Christian souls, I pray God. God buy you.   [*Exit.*]

LAER. Do you see this, O God?

KING. Laertes, I must commune with your grief,   195
Or you deny me right. Go but apart,
Make choice of whom your wisest friends you will,
And they shall hear and judge 'twixt you and me.
If by direct or by collateral hand
They find us touched, we will our kingdom give,   200
Our crown, our life, and all that we call ours,
To you in satisfaction; but if not,
Be you content to lend your patience to us,
And we shall jointly labor with your soul
To give it due content.

LAER.   Let this be so.   205

---

suggests that Ophelia gives rosemary (emblematic
of remembrance) and pansies (of thoughts) to
Laertes; that she gives fennel and columbines (both
signifying marital infidelity) to the Queen; she gives
rue (for repentance) to the King (keeping some for
herself as a sign of her sorrow, but noting that the
King is to wear his rue with *a difference*, an heraldic term designating a mark for distinguishing one
branch of a family from another in a coat-of-arms).

The daisy, an emblem of love's victims, is given to
the King as substitute for the absent Hamlet, whose
absence he has caused. The King would also be
given the violets (emblems of faithfulness, associated both with Ophelia's love for Hamlet, and Polonius's service to the state, both now lost) were
these still available. Each gift of flowers represents
a symbolic reproach to the recipient.
189. *poll* head.

His means of death, his obscure funeral—
No trophy, sword, nor hatchment, o'er his bones,
No noble rite nor formal ostentation—
Cry to be heard, as 'twere from heaven to earth,
That I must call't in question.
KING.   So you shall;   210
And where th' offence is, let the great axe fall.
I pray you go with me.   *Exeunt.*

[IV.vi]

      Enter HORATIO *and* OTHERS.
HOR.   What are they that would speak with me?
GENTLEMEN.   Sea-faring men, sir. They say they have letters for you.
HOR.   Let them come in.   [*Exit* GENTLEMAN.]
    I do not know from what part of the world
    I should be greeted, if not from Lord Hamlet.   5

      Enter SAILORS.
SAIL.   God bless you, sir.
HOR.   Let him bless thee too.
SAIL.   'A shall, sir, an't please him. There's a letter for you, sir—it
    came from th' ambassador that was bound for England—if your
    name be Horatio, as I am let to know it is.   10
HOR.   [*Reads*]. 'Horatio, when thou shalt have overlooked this, give
    these fellows some means to the king. They have letters for him.
    Ere we were two days old at sea, a pirate of very warlike appoint-
    ment gave us chase. Finding ourselves too slow of sail, we put on
    a compelled valor, and in the grapple I boarded them. On the   15
    instant they got clear of our ship, so I alone became their prisoner.
    They have dealt with me like thieves of mercy, but they knew what
    they did; I am to do a good turn for them. Let the king have the
    letters I have sent, and repair thou to me with as much speed as
    thou wouldest fly death. I have words to speak in thine ear will   20
    make thee dumb; yet are they much too light for the bore of the
    matter. These good fellows will bring thee where I am. Rosen-
    crantz and Guildenstern hold their course for England. Of them I
    have much to tell thee. Farewell.
                He that thou knowest thine, HAMLET.'   25
Come, I will give you way for these your letters,
And do't the speedier that you may direct me
To him from whom you brought them.   *Exeunt.*

---

207. *hatchment* coat of arms.   [IV.vi] 21. *bore* literally, caliber of a gun; hence,
                                                    size, importance.

[IV.vii]

Enter KING *and* LAERTES.

KING.   Now must your conscience my acquittance seal,
  And you must put me in your heart for friend,
  Sith you have heard, and with a knowing ear,
  That he which hath your noble father slain
  Pursued my life.
LAER.   It well appears. But tell me   5
  Why you proceeded not against these feats,
  So criminal and so capital in nature,
  As by your safety, greatness, wisdom, all things else,
  You mainly were stirred up.
KING.   O, for two special reasons,
  Which may to you, perhaps, seem much unsinewed,   10
  But yet to me th' are strong. The queen his mother
  Lives almost by his looks, and for myself—
  My virtue or my plague, be it either which—
  She is so conjunctive to my life and soul
  That, as the star moves not but in his sphere,   15
  I could not but by her. The other motive,
  Why to a public count I might not go,
  Is the great love the general gender bear him,
  Who, dipping all his faults in their affection,
  Work like the spring that turneth wood to stone,   20
  Convert his gyves to graces; so that my arrows,
  Too slightly timbered for so loud a wind,
  Would have reverted to my bow again,
  But not where I had aimed them.
LAER.   And so have I a noble father lost,   25
  A sister driven into desp'rate terms,
  Whose worth, if praises may go back again,
  Stood challenger on mount of all the age
  For her perfections. But my revenge will come.
KING.   Break not your sleeps for that. You must not think   30
  That we are made of stuff so flat and dull
  That we can let our beard be shook with danger,
  And think it pastime. You shortly shall hear more.
  I loved you father, and we love our self,
  And that, I hope, will teach you to imagine—   35

    Enter a MESSENGER *with letters.*
MESS.   These to your majesty; this to the queen.

[IV.vii] 7. *capital* punishable by death.
10. *unsinewed* weak.
14. *conjunctive* closely joined.
17. *count* reckoning.

18. *general gender* common people.
21. *gyves* fetters.
35. Following the entrance of the Messenger, the
King says in F "How now? What Newes?" and the

KING.   From Hamlet! Who brought them?

MESS.   Sailors, my lord, they say. I saw them not.
They were given me by Claudio; he received them
Of him that brought them.

KING.   Laertes, you shall hear them.—   40
Leave us.   [*Exit* MESSENGER.]
[*Reads.*] 'High and mighty, you shall know I am set naked on
your kingdom. To-morrow shall I beg leave to see your kingly eyes,
when I shall, first asking your pardon, thereunto recount the occasion of my sudden and more strange return.

HAMLET.' 45

What should this mean? Are all the rest come back?
Or is it some abuse, and no such thing?

LAER.   Know you the hand?

KING.   'Tis Hamlet's character. 'Naked'!
And in a postscript here, he says 'alone'.   50
Can you devise me?

LAER.   I am lost in it, my lord. But let him come.
It warms the very sickness in my heart
That I shall live and tell him to his teeth
'Thus didest thou.'

KING.   If it be so, Laertes—   55
As how should it be so, how otherwise?—
Will you be ruled by me?

LAER.   Ay, my lord,
So you will not o'errule me to a peace.

KING.   To thine own peace. If he be now returned,
As checking at his voyage, and that he means   60
No more to undertake it, I will work him
To an exploit now ripe in my device,
Under the which he shall not choose but fall;
And for his death no wind of blame shall breathe
But even his mother shall uncharge the practice   65
And call it accident.

LAER.   My lord, I will be ruled;
The rather if you could devise it so
That I might be the organ.

KING.   It falls right.
You have been talked of since your travel much,

Messenger replies, "Letters my Lord from *Ham-let.*" Jenkins comments (*SB* 13.36): "In *Q* the King is not told the letters come from Hamlet; he is left to find this out as he reads, and his cry 'From *Hamlet*' betokens his astonishment on doing so. I think Hamlet would not have approved of the F messenger who robs his bomb of the full force of its explosion. Shakespeare's messenger did not even know he carried such a bomb, for the letters had reached him via sailors who were ignorant of their sender. They took him for 'th' Embassador that was bound for *England*' (IV.vi.9). F, with its too knowledgeable messenger, by seeking to enhance the effect, destroys it."

51. *devise* explain to.

60. *checking at* turning aside from (like a falcon turning from its quarry for other prey).

65. *uncharge the practice* regard the deed as free from villainy.

68. *organ* instrument.

And that in Hamlet's hearing, for a quality   70
Wherein they say you shine. Your sum of parts
Did not together pluck such envy from him
As did that one, and that, in my regard,
Of the unworthiest siege.
LAER.   What part is that, my lord?
KING.   A very riband in the cap of youth,   75
Yet needful too, for youth no less becomes
The light and careless livery that it wears
Than settled age his sables and his weeds,
Importing health and graveness. Two months since
Here was a gentleman of Normandy.   80
I have seen myself, and served against, the French,
And they can well on horseback, but this gallant
Had witchcraft in't. He grew unto his seat,
And to such wondrous doing brought his horse,
As had he been incorpsed and demi-natured   85
With the brave beast. So far he topped my thought
That I, in forgery of shapes and tricks,
Come short of what he did.
LAER.   A Norman was't?
KING.   A Norman.
LAER.   Upon my life, Lamord.
KING.   The very same.   90
LAER.   I know him well. He is the brooch indeed
And gem of all the nation.
KING.   He made confession of you,
And gave you such a masterly report
For art and exercise in your defence,   95
And for your rapier most especial,
That he cried out 'twould be a sight indeed
If one could match you. The scrimers of their nation
He swore had neither motion, guard, nor eye,
If you opposed them. Sir, this report of his   100
Did Hamlet so envenom with his envy
That he could nothing do but wish and beg
Your sudden coming o'er, to play with you.
Now out of this—
LAER.   What out of this, my lord?
KING.   Laertes, was your father dear to you?   105
Or are you like the painting of a sorrow,
A face without a heart?
LAER.   Why ask you this?

---

74. *siege* rank.
78. *weeds* garments.
85. *incorpsed* made one body; *demi-natured* like a
centaur, half man half horse.

86. *topped* excelled.
87. *forgery* invention.
98. *scrimers* fencers (French *escrimeurs*).

KING.   Not that I think you did not love your father,
    But that I know love is begun by time,
    And that I see in passages of proof,   110
    Time qualifies the spark and fire of it.
    There lives within the very flame of love
    A kind of wick or snuff that will abate it,
    And nothing is at a like goodness still,
    For goodness, growing to a plurisy,   115
    Dies in his own too much. That we would do,
    We should do when we would; for this 'would' changes,
    And hath abatements and delays as many
    As there are tongues, are hands, are accidents,
    And then this 'should' is like a spendthrift's sigh   120
    That hurts by easing. But to the quick of th' ulcer—
    Hamlet comes back; what would you undertake
    To show yourself in deed your father's son
    More than in words?
LAER.   To cut his throat i' th' church.
KING.   No place indeed should murder sanctuarize;   125
    Revenge should have no bounds. But good Laertes,
    Will you do this, keep close within your chamber;
    Hamlet returned shall know you are come home;
    We'll put on those shall praise your excellence,
    And set a double varnish on the fame   130
    The Frenchman gave you, bring you in fine together,
    And wager on your heads. He, being remiss,
    Most generous, and free from all contriving,
    Will not peruse the foils, so that with ease,
    Or with a little shuffling, you may choose   135
    A sword unbated, and in a pass of practice
    Requite him for your father.
LAER.   I will do't,
    And for that purpose I'll anoint my sword.
    I bought an unction of a mountebank
    So mortal that but dip a knife in it,   140
    Where it draws blood no cataplasm so rare,
    Collected from all simples that have virtue
    Under the moon, can save the thing from death
    That is but scratched withal. I'll touch my point
    With this contagion, that if I gall him slightly,   145
    It may be death.
KING.   Let's further think of this,

110. *passages of proof* incidents of experience.
111. *qualifies* weakens.
115. *plurisy* excess.
121. *quick* sensitive flesh.
125. *sanctuarize* give sanctuary to.
132. *remiss* careless.

134. *peruse* inspect.
136. *unbated* not blunted; *pass of practice* treacherous thrust.
141. *cataplasm* poultice.
142. *simples* medicinal herbs.

Weigh what convenience both of time and means
May fit us to our shape. If this should fail,
And that our drift look through our bad performance,
'Twere better not assayed. Therefore this project   150
Should have a back or second that might hold
If this did blast in proof. Soft, let me see.
We'll make a solemn wager on your cunnings—
I ha't.
When in your motion you are hot and dry—   155
As make your bouts more violent to that end—
And that he calls for drink, I'll have preferred him
A chalice for the nonce, whereon but sipping,
If he by chance escape your venomed stuck,
Our purpose may hold there.—But stay, what noise?   160

     Enter QUEEN.
QUEEN.   One woe doth tread upon another's heel,
So fast they follow. Your sister's drowned, Laertes.
LAER.   Drowned? O, where?
QUEEN.   There is a willow grows askant the brook
That shows his hoar leaves in the glassy stream.   165
Therewith fantastic garlands did she make
Of crowflowers, nettles, daisies, and long purples
That liberal shepherds give a grosser name,
But our cold maids do dead men's fingers call them.
There on the pendent boughs her crownet weeds   170
Clamb'ring to hang, an envious sliver broke,
When down her weedy trophies and herself
Fell in the weeping brook. Her clothes spread wide,
And mermaid-like awhile they bore her up,
Which time she chanted snatches of old lauds,   175
As one incapable of her own distress,
Or like a creature native and indued
Unto that element. But long it could not be
Till that her garments, heavy with their drink,
Pulled the poor wretch from her melodious lay   180
To muddy death.
LAER.   Alas, then she is drowned?
QUEEN.   Drowned, drowned.
LAER.   Too much of water hast thou, poor Ophelia,

148. *shape* plan.
149. *drift* scheme.
151. *back or second* something in support.
152. *blast in proof* burst during trial (like a faulty cannon).
155. *motion* exertion.
157. *preferred* offered to.
158. *nonce* occasion.
159. *stuck* thrust.

164. *askant* alongside.
165. *hoar* gray.
168. *liberal* free-spoken, licentious.
169. *cold* chaste.
170. *crownet* coronet.
171. *envious* malicious.
175. *lauds* hymns.
176. *incapable of* insensible to.
177. *indued* endowed.

And therefore I forbid my tears; but yet
It is our trick; nature her custom holds,   185
Let shame say what it will. When these are gone,
The woman will be out. Adieu, my lord.
I have a speech o' fire that fain would blaze
But that this folly drowns it.   *Exit.*

KING.   Let's follow, Gertrude.
How much I had to do to calm his rage!   190
Now fear I this will give it start again;
Therefore let's follow.   *Exeunt.*

[V.i]

Enter two CLOWNS.

CLOWN.   Is she to be buried in Christian burial when she wilfully
seeks her own salvation?

OTHER.   I tell thee she is, therefore make her grave straight. The
crowner hath sat on her, and finds it Christian burial.

CLOWN.   How can that be, unless she drowned herself in her own   5
defence?

OTHER.   Why, 'tis found so.

CLOWN.   It must be 'se offendendo', it cannot be else. For here lies
the point: if I drown myself wittingly, it argues an act, and an act
hath three branches—it is to act, to do, to perform; argal, she   10
drowned herself wittingly.

OTHER.   Nay, but hear you, Goodman Delver.

CLOWN.   Give me leave. Here lies the water; good. Here stands the
man; good. If the man go to this water and drown himself, it is,
will he, nill he, he goes—mark you that. But if the water come to   15
him and drown him, he drowns not himself. Argal, he that is not
guilty of his own death shortens not his own life.

OTHER.   But is this law?

CLOWN.   Ay, marry, is't; crowner's quest law.

OTHER.   Will you ha' the truth on't? If this had not been a gentle-   20
woman, she should have been buried out o' Christian burial.

CLOWN.   Why, there thou say'st. And the more pity that great folk
should have count'nance in this world to drown or hang themselves more than their even-Christen. Come, my spade. There is
no ancient gentlemen but gard'ners, ditchers, and grave-makers.   25
They hold up Adam's profession.

OTHER.   Was he a gentleman?

CLOWN.   'A was the first that ever bore arms.

OTHER.   Why, he had none.

---

187. *woman* unmanly part of nature.

[V.i] 0.1 CLOWNS rustics.
4. *crowner* coroner.
8. *se offendendo* the Clown's blunder for *se defen-*

dendo ("in self-defense").
10. *argal* therefore (corrupt form of *ergo*).
19. *quest* inquest.
24. *even-Christen* fellow Christian.

CLOWN.   What, art a heathen? How dost thou understand the Scrip- 30
ture? The Scripture says Adam digged. Could he dig without arms?
I'll put another question to thee. If thou answerest me not to the
purpose, confess thyself—
OTHER.   Go to.
CLOWN.   What is he that builds stronger than either the mason, the 35
shipwright, or the carpenter?
OTHER.   The gallows-maker, for that frame outlives a thousand ten-
ants.
CLOWN.   I like thy wit well, in good faith. The gallows does well. But
how does it well? It does well to those that do ill. Now thou dost 40
ill to say the gallows is built stronger than the church. Argal, the
gallows may do well to thee. To't again, come.
OTHER.   Who builds stronger than a mason, a shipwright, or a car-
penter?
CLOWN.   Ay tell me that, and unyoke.   45
OTHER.   Marry, now I can tell.
CLOWN.   To't.
OTHER.   Mass, I cannot tell.

   Enter HAMLET *and* HORATIO *afar off.*
CLOWN.   Cudgel thy brains no more about it, for your dull ass will
not mend his pace with beating. And when you are asked this 50
question next, say 'a grave-maker.' The houses he makes lasts till
doomsday. Go, get thee in, and fetch me a stoup of liquor.
              [*Exit* OTHER CLOWN.]
  [HAMLET *and* HORATIO *come forward as* CLOWN *digs and sings.*]
   In youth, when I did love, did love,   (*Song.*)
    Methought it was very sweet,
   To contract-O-the time for-a-my behove, 55
    O, methought there-a-was nothing-a-meet.
HAM.   Has this fellow no feeling of his business, that 'a sings in grave-
making?
HOR.   Custom hath made it in him a property of easiness.
HAM.   'Tis e'en so. The hand of little employment hath the daintier 60
sense.
CLOWN.   But age, with his stealing steps, (*Song.*)
    Hath clawed me in his clutch,
   And hath shipped me into the land,
    As if I had never been such. 65
         [*Throws up a skull.*]

45. *tell me that, and unyoke* answer the question and then you can relax.
52. *stoup* tankard.
55. *behove* benefit.
55–56. The repeated *a* and *o* may represent the Clown's vocal embellishments, but more probably they represent his grunting as he takes breath in the course of his digging.
59. *a property of easiness* a habit that comes easily to him.

HAM.   That skull had a tongue in it, and could sing once. How the
knave jowls it to the ground, as if 'twere Cain's jawbone, that
did the first murder! This might be the pate of a politician, which
this ass now o'erreaches; one that would circumvent God, might it
not?   70

HOR.   It might, my lord.

HAM.   Or of a courtier, which could say, 'Good morrow, sweet lord!
How does thou, sweet lord?' This might be my Lord Such-a-one,
that praised my Lord Such-a-one's horse, when 'a went to beg it,
might it not?   75

HOR.   Ay, my lord.

HAM.   Why, e'en so, and now my Lady Worm's, chopless, and
knock'd abut the mazzard with a sexton's spade. Here's fine revo-
lution, an we had the trick to see't. Did these bones cost no more
the breeding but to play at loggats with them? Mine ache to think   80
on't.

CLOWN.   A pick-axe and a spade, a spade,   (Song.)
                              For and a shrouding sheet:
                              O, a pit of clay for to be made
                              For such a guest is meet.   85
                                               [Throws up another skull.]

HAM.   There's another. Why may not that be the skull of a lawyer?
Where be his quiddities now, his quillets, his cases, his tenures,
and his tricks? Why does he suffer this mad knave now to knock
him about the sconce with a dirty shovel, and will not tell him of
his action of battery? Hum! This fellow might be in's time a great   90
buyer of land, with his statutes, his recognizances, his fines, his
double vouchers, his recoveries. Is this the fine of his fines, and
the recovery of his recoveries, to have his fine pate full of fine dirt?
Will his vouchers vouch him no more of his purchases, and double ones too, than the length and breadth of a pair of indentures?   95
The very conveyances of his lands will scarcely lie in this box, and
must th' inheritor himself have no more, ha?

HOR.   Not a jot more, my lord.

HAM.   Is not parchment made of sheepskins?

HOR.   Ay, my lord, and of calves' skins too.   100

HAM.   They are sheep and calves which seek out assurance in that.
    I will speak to this fellow. Whose grave's this, sirrah?

CLOWN.   Mine, sir.

67. *jowls* hurls.
69. *circumvent* cheat.
77. *chopless* with lower jaw missing.
78. *mazzard* head.
80. *loggats* small logs of wood for throwing at a
mark.
87. *quiddities* subtle distinctions; *quillets* quib-
bles.

91. *recognizances* legal bonds, defining debts
92. *vouchers* persons vouched or called on to warrant a title.
92. *recoveries* legal processes to break an entail.
95. *pair of indentures* deed or legal agreement in
duplicate.
96. *conveyances* deeds by which property is trans-
ferred.

[*Sings.*] O, a pit of clay for to be made—

HAM.   I think it be thine indeed, for thou liest in't.   105

CLOWN.   You lie out on't, sir, and therefore 'tis not yours. For my
part, I do not lie in't, yet it is mine.

HAM.   Thou dost lie in't, to be in't and say it is thine. 'Tis for the
dead, not for the quick; therefore thou liest.

CLOWN.   'Tis a quick lie, sir; 'twill away again from me to you.   110

HAM.   What man dost thou dig it for?

CLOWN.   For no man, sir.

HAM.   What woman, then?

CLOWN.   For none neither.

HAM.   Who is to be buried in't?   115

CLOWN.   One that was a woman, sir; but, rest her soul, she's dead.

HAM.   How absolute the knave is! We must speak by the card, or
equivocation will undo us. By the Lord, Horatio, this three years
I have took note of it, the age is grown so picked that the toe of the
peasant comes so near the heel of the courtier, he galls his kibe.   120
How long hast thou been grave-maker?

CLOWN.   Of all the days i' th' year, I came to't that day that our last
King Hamlet overcame Fortinbras.

HAM.   How long is that since?

CLOWN.   Cannot you tell that? Every fool can tell that. It was that   125
very day that young Hamlet was born—he that is mad, and sent
into England.

HAM.   Ay, marry, why was he sent into England?

CLOWN.   Why, because 'a was mad. 'A shall recover his wits there;
or, if 'a do not, 'tis no great matter there.   130

HAM.   Why?

CLOWN.   'Twill not be seen in him there. There the men are as mad
as he.

HAM.   How came he mad?

CLOWN.   Very strangely, they say.   135

HAM.   How strangely?

CLOWN.   Faith, e'en with losing his wits.

HAM.   Upon what ground?

CLOWN.   Why, here in Denmark. I have been sexton here, man and
boy, thirty years.   140

HAM.   How long will a man lie i' th' earth ere he rot?

CLOWN.   Faith, if 'a be not rotten before 'a die—as we have many
pocky corses now-a-days that will scarce hold the laying in—'a will
last you some eight year or nine year. A tanner will last you nine
year.   145

HAM.   Why he more than another?

---

117. *absolute* positive; *card* card on which the
points of the mariner's compass are marked (i.e.,
absolutely to the point).

119. *picked* fastidious.
120. *kibe* chilblain.
143. *pocky* infected with pox (syphillis).

CLOWN. Why, sir, his hide is so tanned with his trade that 'a will
keep out water a great while; and your water is a sore decayer of
your whoreson dead body. Here's a skull now hath lien you i' th'
earth three and twenty years.   150

HAM. Whose was it?

CLOWN. A whoreson mad fellow's it was. Whose do you think it
was?

HAM. Nay, I know not.

CLOWN. A pestilence on him for a mad rogue! 'A poured a flagon of
Rhenish on my head once. This same skull, sir, was, sir, Yorick's 155
skull, the king's jester.

HAM. [*Takes the skull.*] This?

CLOWN. E'en that.

HAM. Alas, poor Yorick! I knew him, Horatio—a fellow of infinite
jest, of most excellent fancy. He hath bore me on his back a thou- 160
sand times, and now how abhorred in my imagination it is! My
gorge rises at it. Here hung those lips that I have kissed I know not
how oft. Where be your gibes now, your gambols, your songs,
your flashes of merriment that were wont to set the table on a roar?
Not one now to mock your own grinning? Quite chop-fall'n? Now 165
get you to my lady's chamber, and tell her, let her paint an inch
thick, to this favor she must come. Make her laugh at that. Prithee, Horatio, tell me one thing.

HOR. What's that, my lord?

HAM. Dost thou think Alexander looked o' this fashion i' th' earth? 170

HOR. E'en so.

HAM. And smelt so? Pah!   [*Throws down the skull.*]

HOR. E'en so, my lord.

HAM. To what base uses we may return, Horatio! Why may not
imagination trace the noble dust of Alexander till 'a find it stopping 175
a bung-hole?

HOR. 'Twere to consider too curiously to consider so.

HAM. No, faith, not a jot, but to follow him thither with modesty
enough, and likelihood to lead it. Alexander died, Alexander was
buried, Alexander returneth to dust; the dust is earth; of earth we 180
make loam; and why of that loam whereto he was converted might
they not stop a beer-barrel?

> Imperious Cæsar, dead and turned to clay,
> Might stop a hole to keep the wind away.
> O, that that earth which kept the world in awe   185
> Should patch a wall t'expel the winter's flaw!

---

155. *Rhenish* Rhine wine.   186. *flaw* gust.
177. *too curiously* over ingeniously.

But soft, but soft awhile! Here comes the king,
The queen, the courtiers.

Enter KING, QUEEN, LAERTES, *and the Corse* [*with a Doctor*
of Divinity as PRIEST *and* LORDS *attendant*].
                     Who is this they follow?
And with such maiméd rites? This doth betoken
The corse they follow did with desperate hand   190
Fordo it own life. 'Twas of some estate.
Couch we awhile and mark.   [*Retires with* HORATIO.]
LAER.   What ceremony else?
HAM.   That is Laertes, a very noble youth. Mark.
LAER.   What ceremony else?   195
DOCTOR.   Her obsequies have been as far enlarged
  As we have warranty. Her death was doubtful,
  And but that great command o'ersways the order,
  She should in ground unsanctified been lodged
  Till the last trumpet. For charitable prayers,   200
  Shards, flints, and pebbles, should be thrown on her.
  Yet here she is allowed her virgin crants,
  Her maiden strewments, and the bringing home
  Of bell and burial.
LAER.   Must there no more be done?
DOCTOR.   No more be done.   205
  We should profane the service of the dead
  To sing a requiem and such rest to her
  As to peace-parted souls.
LAER.   Lay her i' th' earth,
  And from her fair and unpolluted flesh
  May violets spring! I tell thee, churlish priest,   210
  A minist'ring angel shall my sister be
  When thou liest howling.
HAM.   What, the fair Ophelia!
QUEEN.   Sweets to the sweet. Farewell!   [*Scatters flowers.*]
  I hoped thou shouldst have been my Hamlet's wife.
  I thought thy bride-bed to have decked, sweet maid, 215
  And not have strewed thy grave.
LAER.   O, treble woe
  Fall ten times treble on that curséd head
  Whose wicked deed thy most ingenious sense
  Deprived thee of! Hold off the earth awhile,
  Till I have caught her once more in mine arms.   220
                     [*Leaps into the grave.*]

---

191. *Fordo* destroy; *it* its.   202. *crants* garland.
201. *Shards* bits of broken pottery.   218. *most ingenious* of quickest apprehension.

Now pile your dust upon the quick and dead,
Till of this flat a mountain you have made
T' o'er-top old Pelion or the skyish head
Of blue Olympus.
HAM. [*Coming forward.*] What is he whose grief
  Bears such an emphasis, whose phrase of sorrow   225
  Conjures the wand'ring stars, and makes them stand
  Like wonder-wounded hearers? This is I,
  Hamlet the Dane.
           [LAERTES *climbs out of the grave.*]
LAER. The devil take thy soul!   [*Grappling with him.*]
HAM.   Thou pray'st not well.
  I prithee take thy fingers from my throat,   230
  For though I am not splenitive and rash,
  Yet have I in me something dangerous,
  Which let thy wisdom fear. Hold off thy hand.
KING. Pluck them asunder.
QUEEN. Hamlet! Hamlet!   235
ALL. Gentlemen!
HOR. Good my lord, be quiet.
          [*The* ATTENDANTS *part them.*]
HAM. Why, I will fight with him upon this theme
  Until my eyelids will no longer wag.
QUEEN. O my son, what theme?   240
HAM. I loved Ophelia. Forty thousand brothers
  Could not with all their quantity of love
  Make up my sum. What wilt thou do for her?
KING. O, he is mad, Laertes.
QUEEN. For love of God, forbear him.   245
HAM. 'Swounds, show me what thou't do.
  Woo't weep, woo't fight, woo't fast, woo't tear thyself,
  Woo't drink up eisel, eat a crocodile?
  I'll do't. Dost come here to whine?
  To outface me with leaping in her grave?   250
  Be buried quick with her, and so will I.
  And if thou prate of mountains, let them throw
  Millions of acres on us, till our ground,
  Singeing his pate against the burning zone,
  Make Ossa like a wart! Nay, an thou'lt mouth,   255
  I'll rant as well as thou.
QUEEN.   This is mere madness;

---

223. *Pelion* a mountain in Thessaly, like Olympus, line 224, and Ossa, line 255 (the allusion is to the war in which the Titans fought the gods and, in their attempt to scale heaven, heaped Ossa and Olympus on Pelion, or Pelion and Ossa on Olympus).

225. *such an emphasis* so vehement an expression or display.
231. *splenitive* fiery-tempered (from the spleen, seat of anger).
247. *Woo't* wilt (thou).
248. *eisel* vinegar.

And thus awhile the fit will work on him.
Anon, as patient as the female dove
When that her golden couplets are disclosed,
His silence will sit drooping.
HAM. 　　　　　　　　　　Hear you, sir. 　　　　260
　　What is the reason that you use me thus?
　　I loved you ever. But it is no matter.
　　Let Hercules himself do what he may,
　　The cat will mew, and dog will have his day.
KING. 　I pray thee, good Horatio, wait upon him. 　　　265
　　　　　　　　　　　　　Exit Hamlet and Horatio.
[*To* LAERTES.] Strengthen your patience in our last night's speech.
We'll put the matter to the present push.—
Good Gertrude, set some watch over your son.—
This grave shall have a living monument.
An hour of quiet shortly shall we see; 　　　　　270
Till then in patience our proceeding be. 　　　　*Exeunt.*

[V.ii]

　　　　　　　Enter HAMLET *and* HORATIO.
HAM. 　So much for this, sir; now shall you see the other.
　　You do remember all the circumstance?
HOR. 　Remember it, my lord!
HAM. 　Sir, in my heart there was a kind of fighting
　　That would not let me sleep. Methought I lay 　　5
　　Worse than the mutines in the bilboes. Rashly,
　　And praised be rashness for it—let us know,
　　Our indiscretion sometime serves us well,
　　When our deep plots do pall; and that should learn us
　　There's a divinity that shapes our ends, 　　　10
　　Rough-hew them how we will—
HOR. 　　　　　　　　　That is most certain.
HAM. 　Up from my cabin,
　　My sea-gown scarfed about me, in the dark
　　Groped I to find out them, had my desire,
　　Fingered their packet, and in fine withdrew 　　15
　　To mine own room again, making so bold,
　　My fears forgetting manners, to unseal
　　Their grand commission; where I found, Horatio—
　　Ah, royal knavery!—an exact command,
　　Larded with many several sorts of reasons, 　　20
　　Importing Denmark's health, and England's too,

259. *couplets* newly-hatched pair.

[V.ii] 6. *mutines* mutineers; *bilboes* fetters.

9. *pall* fail.
15. *Fingered* filched.
20. *Larded* garnished.

With, ho! such bugs and goblins in my life,
That on the supervise, no leisure bated,
No, not to stay the grinding of the axe,
My head should be struck off.
HOR.   Is't possible?   25
HAM.   Here's the commission; read it at more leisure.
But wilt thou hear now how I did proceed?
HOR.   I beseech you.
HAM.   Being thus benetted round with villainies,
Or I could make a prologue to my brains,   30
They had begun the play. I sat me down,
Devised a new commission, wrote it fair.
I once did hold it, as our statists do,
A baseness to write fair, and labored much
How to forget that learning; but sir, now   35
It did me yeoman's service. Wilt thou know
Th' effect of what I wrote?
HOR.   Ay, good my lord.
HAM.   An earnest conjuration from the king,
As England was his faithful tributary,
As love between them like the palm might flourish,   40
As peace should still her wheaten garland wear
And stand a comma 'tween their amities,
And many such like as's of great charge,
That on the view and knowing of these contents,
Without debatement further more or less,   45
He should those bearers put to sudden death,
Not shriving-time allowed.
HOR.   How was this sealed?
HAM.   Why, even in that was heaven ordinant,
I had my father's signet in my purse,
Which was the model of that Danish seal,   50
Folded the writ up in the form of th' other,
Subscribed it, gave't th' impression, placed it safely,
The changeling never known. Now, the next day
Was our sea-fight, and what to this was sequent
Thou knowest already.   55
HOR.   So Guildenstern and Rosencrantz go to't.
HAM.   Why, man, they did make love to this employment.
They are not near my conscience; their defeat
Does by their own insinuation grow.

22. *bugs and goblins* imaginary horrors (here, horrendous crimes attributed to Hamlet, and represented as dangers should he be allowed to live).
23. *supervise* perusal; *bated* deducted, allowed.
24. *stay* await.
30. *Or* ere.
33. *statists* statesmen.

42. *comma* a connective that also acknowledges separateness.
43. *charge* (1) importance (2) burden (the double meaning fits the play that makes "as's" into "asses").
48. *ordinant* guiding.
52. *Subscribed* signed.
59. *insinuation* intrusion.

'Tis dangerous when the baser nature comes   60
Between the pass and fell incensèd points
Of mighty opposites.
HOR.   Why, what a king is this!
HAM.   Does it not, think thee, stand me now upon—
He that hath killed my king and whored my mother,
Popped in between th' election and my hopes,   65
Thrown out his angle for my proper life,
And with such coz'nage—is't not perfect conscience
To quit him with this arm? And is't not to be damned
To let this canker of our nature come
In further evil?   70
HOR.   It must be shortly known to him from England
What is the issue of the business there.
HAM.   It will be short; the interim is mine.
And a man's life's no more than to say 'one'.
But I am very sorry, good Horatio,   75
That to Laertes I forgot myself;
For by the image of my cause I see
The portraiture of his. I'll court his favours.
But sure the bravery of his grief did put me
Into a tow'ring passion.
HOR.   Peace; who comes here?   80

Enter [OSRIC] *a courtier.*

OSR.   Your lordship is right welcome back to Denmark.
HAM.   I humbly thank you, sir. [*Aside to* HORATIO.] Dost know this
water-fly?
HOR.   [*Aside to* HAMLET.] No, my good lord.
HAM.   [*Aside to* HORATIO.] Thy state is the more gracious, for 'tis a   85
vice to know him. He hath much land, and fertile. Let a beast be
lord of beasts, and his crib shall stand at the king's mess. 'Tis a
chough, but as I say, spacious in the possession of dirt.
OSR.   Sweet lord, if your lordship were at leisure, I should impart a
thing to you from his majesty.   90
HAM.   I will receive it, sir, with all diligence of spirit. Put your bon-
net to his right use. 'Tis for the head.
OSR.   I thank your lordship, it is very hot.
HAM.   No, believe me, 'tis very cold; the wind is northerly.
OSR.   It is indifferent cold, my lord, indeed.   95
HAM.   But yet methinks it is very sultry and hot for my complexion.
OSR.   Exceedingly, my lord; it is very sultry, as 'twere—I cannot tell

61. *pass* thrust; *fell* fierce.
63. *Does it not* * * * *stand me now upon* is it not
incumbent upon me.
65. *election* i.e., to the kingship, Denmark being
an elective monarchy.
66. *angle* fishing line; *proper* own.

68. *quit* repay.
79. *bravery* ostentatious display.
87. *mess* table.
88. *chough* jackdaw; thus, a chatterer.
95. *indifferent* somewhat.
96. *complexion* temperament.

how. My lord, his majesty bade me signify to you that 'a has laid
a great wager on your head. Sir, this is the matter—

HAM.   I beseech you, remember.   100

                        [HAMLET *moves him to put on his hat.*]

OSR.   Nay, good my lord; for my ease, in good faith. Sir, here is
newly come to court Laertes; believe me, an absolute gentleman,
full of most excellent differences, of very soft society and great
showing. Indeed, to speak feelingly of him, he is the card or cal-
endar of gentry, for you shall find in him the continent of what 105
part a gentleman would see.

HAM.   Sir, his definement suffers no perdition in you, though I know
to divide him inventorially would dozy th' arithmetic of memory,
and yet but yaw neither in respect of his quick sail. But in the
verity of extolment, I take him to be a soul of great article, and 110
his infusion of such dearth and rareness as, to make true diction
of him, his semblable is his mirror, and who else would trace him,
his umbrage, nothing more.

OSR.   Your lordship speaks most infallibly of him.

HAM.   The concernancy, sir? Why do we wrap the gentleman in our 115
more rawer breath?

OSR.   Sir?

HOR.   Is't not possible to understand in another tongue? You will
to't, sir, really.

HAM.   What imports the nomination of this gentleman?   120

OSR.   Of Laertes?

HOR.   [*Aside.*] His purse is empty already. All's golden words are
spent.

HAM.   Of him, sir.

OSR.   I know you are not ignorant—   125

HAM.   I would you did, sir; yet, in faith, if you did, it would not
much approve me. Well, sir.

OSR.   You are not ignorant of what excellence Laertes is—

HAM.   I dare not confess that, lest I should compare with him in
excellence; but to know a man well were to know himself.   130

OSR.   I mean, sir, for his weapon; but in the imputation laid on him
by them in his meed, he's unfellowed.

HAM.   What's his weapon?

OSR.   Rapier and dagger.

HAM.   That's two of his weapons—but well.   135

103. *differences* distinguishing qualities.
103–4. *great showing* distinguished appearance.
104. *card* map.
105. *continent* all-containing embodiment.
107. *definement* definition.
108. *divide him inventorially* classify him in de-
tail; *dozy* dizzy.
109. *yaw* hold to a course unsteadily like a ship
that steers wild.
110. *article* scope, importance.

111. *infusion* essence; *dearth* scarcity.
112. *semblable* likeness; *trace* (1) draw (2) follow.
113. *umbrage* shadow.
115. *concernancy* import, relevance.
119. *to't* i.e., get to an understanding.
120. *nomination* mention.
127. *approve* commend.
129. *compare* compete.
132. *meed* pay; *unfellowed* unequaled.

OSR.   The king, sir, hath wagered with him six Barbary horses, against
the which he has impawned, as I take it, six French rapiers and
poniards, with their assigns, as girdle, hangers, and so. Three of
the carriages, in faith, are very dear to fancy, very responsive to the
hilts, most delicate carriages, and of very liberal conceit.   140

HAM.   What call you the carriages?

HOR.   [*Aside to* HAMLET.] I knew you must be edified by the margent
ere you had done.

OSR.   The carriages, sir, are the hangers.

HAM.   The phrase would be more germane to the matter if we could 145
carry a cannon by our sides. I would it might be hangers till then.
But on! Six Barbary horses against six French swords, their assigns,
and three liberal conceited carriages; that's the French bet against
the Danish. Why is this all impawned, as you call it?

OSR.   The king, sir, hath laid, sir, that in a dozen passes between 150
yourself and him he shall not exceed you three hits; he hath laid
on twelve for nine, and it would come to immediate trial if your
lordship would vouchsafe the answer.

HAM.   How if I answer no?

OSR.   I mean, my lord, the opposition of your person in trial.   155

HAM.   Sir, I will walk here in the hall. If it please his majesty, it is
the breathing time of day with me. Let the foils be brought, the
gentleman willing, and the king hold his purpose; I will win for
him an I can. If not, I will gain nothing but my shame and the
odd hits.   160

OSR.   Shall I deliver you so?

HAM.   To this effect, sir, after what flourish your nature will.

OSR.   I commend my duty to your lordship.

HAM.   Yours. [*Exit* OSRIC.] He does well to commend it himself;
there are no tongues else for's turn.   165

HOR.   This lapwing runs away with the shell on his head.

HAM.   'A did comply, sir, with his dug before 'a sucked it. Thus has
he, and many more of the same bevy that I know the drossy age
dotes on, only got the tune of the time; and out of an habit of
encounter, a kind of yesty collection which carries them through 170

---

137. *impawned* staked.

138. *assigns* appendages.

140. *carriages* an affected word for *hangers*, i.e.,
straps from which the weapon was hung; *liberal
conceit* elaborate design.

142. *margent* margin (where explanatory notes were
printed).

150–51. *in a dozen passes . . . he shall not exceed
you three hits* the odds the King proposes seem to
be that in a match of twelve bouts, Hamlet will
win at least five. Laertes would need to win by at
least eight to four.

151–52. *he hath laid on twelve for nine* "he" apparently is Laertes, who has seemingly raised the

odds against himself by wagering that out of twelve
bouts he will win nine.

157. *breathing time* time for taking exercise.

159. *an* if.

166. *lapwing* a bird reputedly so precocious as to
run as soon as hatched.

167. *comply* observe the formalities of courtesy; *dug*
mother's nipple.

168. *bevy* a covey of quails or lapwings.

168. *drossy* frivolous.

170. *encounter* manner of address or accosting;
yesty collection a frothy and superficial patchwork
of terms from the conversation of others.

and through the most fanned and winnowed opinions; and do but
blow them to their trial, the bubbles are out.

     Enter a LORD.

LORD.   My lord, his majesty commended him to you by young Osric,
   who brings back to him that you attend him in the hall. He sends
   to know if your pleasure hold to play with Laertes, or that you will 175
   take longer time.

HAM.   I am constant to my purposes; they follow the king's pleasure.
   If his fitness speaks, mine is ready; now or whensoever, provided I
   be so able as now.

LORD.   The king and queen and all are coming down.   180

HAM.   In happy time.

LORD.   The queen desires you to use some gentle entertainment to
   Laertes before you fall to play.

HAM.   She well instructs me.   [*Exit* LORD.]

HOR.   You will lose, my lord.   185

HAM.   I do not think so. Since he went into France I have been in
   continual practice. I shall win at the odds. But thou wouldst not
   think how ill all's here about my heart. But it is no matter.

HOR.   Nay, good my lord—

HAM.   It is but foolery, but it is such a kind of gaingiving as would 190
   perhaps trouble a woman.

HOR.   If your mind dislike anything, obey it. I will forestall their
   repair hither, and say you are not fit.

HAM.   Not a whit, we defy augury. There is special providence in
   the fall of a sparrow. If it be now, 'tis not to come; if it be not to 195
   come, it will be now; if it be not now, yet it will come. The read-
   iness is all. Since no man of aught he leaves knows, what is't to
   leave betimes? Let be.

   A *table prepared.* [*Enter*] TRUMPETS, DRUMS, *and* OFFICERS *with*
   cushions; KING, QUEEN, [OSRIC] *and all the* STATE, [*with*] *foils, dag-*
   gers, *and* LAERTES.

KING.   Come, Hamlet, come, and take this hand from me.
         [*The* KING *puts* LAERTES' *hand into* HAMLET'*s.*]

HAM.   Give me your pardon, sir. I have done you wrong,   200
   But pardon 't as you are a gentleman.
   This presence knows, and you must needs have heard,
   How I am punished with a sore distraction.
   What I have done
   That might your nature, honor, and exception,   205
   Roughly awake, I here proclaim was madness.
   Was 't Hamlet wronged Laertes? Never Hamlet.
   If Hamlet from himself be ta'en away,

---

171. *winnowed* tested, freed from inferior ele-   178. *fitness* convenience, inclination.
ments.   190. *gaingiving* misgiving.

And when he's not himself does wrong Laertes,
Then Hamlet does it not, Hamlet denies it.   210
Who does it then? His madness. If't be so,
Hamlet is of the faction that is wronged;
His madness is poor Hamlet's enemy.
Sir, in this audience,
Let my disclaiming from a purposed evil   215
Free me so far in your most generous thoughts
That I have shot my arrow o'er the house
And hurt my brother.
LAER.   I am satisfied in nature,
Whose motive in this case should stir me most
To my revenge. But in my terms of honor   220
I stand aloof, and will no reconcilement
Till by some elder masters of known honor
I have a voice and precedent of peace
To keep my name ungored. But till that time
I do receive your offered love like love,   225
And will not wrong it.
HAM.   I embrace it freely,
And will this brother's wager frankly play.
Give us the foils.
LAER.   Come, one for me.
HAM.   I'll be your foil, Laertes. In mine ignorance
Your skill shall, like a star i' th' darkest night,   230
Stick fiery off indeed.
LAER.   You mock me, sir.
HAM.   No, by this hand.
KING.   Give them the foils, young Osric. Cousin Hamlet,
You know the wager?
HAM.   Very well, my lord;
Your Grace has laid the odds o' th' weaker side.   235
KING.   I do not fear it, I have seen you both;
But since he is bettered, we have therefore odds.
LAER.   This is too heavy; let me see another.
HAM.   This likes me well. These foils have all a length?
                                  [*They prepare to play.*]
OSR.   Ay, my good lord.   240
KING.   Set me the stoups of wine upon that table.
If Hamlet give the first or second hit,
Or quit in answer of the third exchange,
Let all the battlements their ordnance fire.
The king shall drink to Hamlet's better breath,   245
And in the cup an union shall he throw,

223. *voice and precedent* authoritative statement justified by precedent.
229. *foil* (1) setting for gem (2) weapon.
237. *bettered* perfected through training.

239. *have all a langth* are all of the same length.
243. *quit in answer* literally, give as good as he gets (i.e., if the third bout is a draw).
246. *union* pearl.

Richer than that which four successive kings
In Denmark's crown have worn. Give me the cups,
And let the kettle to the trumpet speak,
The trumpet to the cannoneer without,   250
The cannons to the heavens, the heaven to earth,
'Now the king drinks to Hamlet'. Come, begin—
                                                Trumpets the while.
And you, the judges, bear a wary eye.
HAM.   Come on, sir.
LAER.   Come, my lord.   [*They play.*]
HAM.   One.
LAER.   No.
HAM.   Judgment.
OSR.   A hit, a very palpable hit.   255
            Drums, trumpets, and shot. Flourish; a piece goes off.
LAER.   Well, again.
KING.   Stay, give me drink. Hamlet, this pearl is thine.
Here's to thy health. Give him the cup.
HAM.   I'll play this bout first; set it by awhile.
Come.   [*They play.*] 260
Another hit; what say you?
LAER.   I do confess't.
KING.   Our son shall win.
QUEEN.   He's fat, and scant of breath.
Here, Hamlet, take my napkin, rub thy brows.
The queen carouses to thy fortune, Hamlet.   265
HAM.   Good madam!
KING.   Gertrude, do not drink.
QUEEN.   I will, my lord; I pray you pardon me.
KING.   [*Aside.*] It is the poisoned cup; it is too late.
HAM.   I dare not drink yet, madam; by and by.   270
QUEEN.   Come, let me wipe thy face.
LAER.   My lord, I'll hit him now.
KING.   I do not think't.
LAER.   [*Aside.*] And yet it is almost against my conscience.
HAM.   Come, for the third, Laertes. You do but dally.
I pray you pass with your best violence;   275
I am afeard you make a wanton of me.
LAER.   Say you so? Come on.   [*They play.*]
OSR.   Nothing, neither way.
LAER.   Have at you now! [LAERTES *wounds* HAMLET; *then, in scuf-*
fling, they change rapiers.]
KING.   Part them. They are incensed.   280
HAM.   Nay, come again.
            [HAMLET *wounds* LAERTES. *The* QUEEN *falls.*]

---

263. *fat* out of training.   276. *make a wanton of me* trifle with me.

OSR.   Look to the queen there, ho!

HOR.   They bleed on both sides. How is it, my lord?

OSR.   How is't, Laertes?

LAER.   Why, as a woodcock to mine own springe, Osric.   285
   I am justly killed with mine own treachery.

HAM.   How does the queen?

KING.   She swoons to see them bleed.

QUEEN.   No, no, the drink, the drink! O my dear Hamlet!
   The drink, the drink! I am poisoned.   [Dies.]

HAM.   O, villainy! Ho! let the door be locked.   290
   Treachery! seek it out.   [LAERTES falls. Exit OSRIC.]

LAER.   It is here, Hamlet. Hamlet, thou art slain;
   No med'cine in the world can do thee good.
   In thee there is not half an hour's life.
   The treacherous instrument is in thy hand,   295
   Unbated and envenomed. The foul practice
   Hath turned itself on me. Lo, here I lie,
   Never to rise again. Thy mother's poisoned.
   I can no more. The king, the king's to blame.

HAM.   The point envenomed too?   300
   Then, venom, to thy work.   [Wounds the KING.]

ALL.   Treason! treason!

KING.   O, yet defend me, friends. I am but hurt.

HAM.   Here, thou incestuous, murd'rous, damnéd Dane,
   Drink off this potion. Is thy union here?   305
   Follow my mother.   [KING dies.]

LAER.   He is justly served.
   It is a poison tempered by himself.
   Exchange forgiveness with me, noble Hamlet.
   Mine and my father's death come not upon thee,
   Nor thine on me!   [Dies.] 310

HAM.   Heaven make thee free of it! I follow thee.
   I am dead, Horatio. Wretched queen, adieu!
   You that look pale and tremble at this chance,
   That are but mutes or audience to this act,
   Had I but time, as this fell sergeant Death   315
   Is strict in his arrest, O, I could tell you—
   But let it be. Horatio, I am dead:
   Thou livest; report me and my cause aright
   To the unsatisfied.

HOR.   Never believe it.
   I am more an antique Roman than a Dane.   320
   Here's yet some liquor left.

HAM.   As th'art a man,
   Give me the cup. Let go. By heaven, I'll ha't.

---

285. *springe* trap.
296. *Unbated* unblunted; *practice* plot.

315. *fell* cruel; *sergeant* an officer whose duty is to summon persons to appear before a court.

O God, Horatio, what a wounded name,
Things standing thus unknown, shall I leave behind me!
If thou didst ever hold me in thy heart,   325
Absent thee from felicity awhile,
And in this harsh world draw thy breath in pain,
To tell my story.   *A march afar off.*
                    What warlike noise is this?
        Enter OSRIC.
OSR.   Young Fortinbras, with conquest come from Poland,
To th' ambassadors of England gives   330
This warlike volley.
HAM.   O, I die, Horatio!
The potent poison quite o'er-crows my spirit.
I cannot live to hear the news from England,
But I do prophesy th' election lights
On Fortinbras. He has my dying voice.   335
So tell him, with th' occurrents, more and less,
Which have solicited—the rest is silence.   [*Dies.*]
HOR.   Now cracks a noble heart. Good night, sweet prince,
And flights of angels sing thee to thy rest!   [*March within.*]
Why does the drum come hither?   340

        Enter FORTINBRAS, *with the* AMBASSADORS [*and with drum,
        colors, and* ATTENDANTS].
FORT.   Where is this sight?
HOR.   What is it you would see?
If aught of woe or wonder, cease your search.
FORT.   This quarry cries on havoc. O proud death,
What feast is toward in thine eternal cell
That thou so many princes at a shot   345
So bloodily hast struck?
AMB.   The sight is dismal;
And our affairs from England come too late.
The ears are senseless that should give us hearing
To tell him his commandment is fulfilled,
That Rosencrantz and Guildenstern are dead.   350
Where should we have our thanks?
HOR.   Not from his mouth,
Had it th' ability of life to thank you.
He never gave commandment for their death.
But since, so jump upon this bloody question,
You from the Polack wars, and you from England,   355
Are here arrived, give order that these bodies

---

332. *o'er-crows* triumphs over.   343. *quarry* pile of dead.
335. *voice* vote.   344. *toward* impending.
336. *more and less* great and small.   354. *jump* exactly.
337. *solicited* incited, prompted.

High on a stage be placéd to the view,
And let me speak to th' yet unknowing world
How these things came about. So shall you hear
Of carnal, bloody, and unnatural acts;   360
Of accidental judgments, casual slaughters;
Of deaths put on by cunning and forced cause;
And, in this upshot, purposes mistook
Fall'n on th' inventors' heads. All this can I
Truly deliver.
FORT.   Let us haste to hear it,   365
And call the noblest to the audience.
For me, with sorrow I embrace my fortune.
I have some rights of memory in this kingdom,
Which now to claim my vantage doth invite me.
HOR.   Of that I shall have also cause to speak,   370
And from his mouth whose voice will draw on more.
But let this same be presently performed,
Even while men's minds are wild, lest more mischance
On plots and errors happen.
FORT.   Let four captains
Bear Hamlet like a soldier to the stage,   375
For he was likely, had he been put on,
To have proved most royal; and for his passage
The soldier's music and the rite of war
Speak loudly for him.
Take up the bodies. Such a sight as this   380
Becomes the field, but here shows much amiss.
Go, bid the soldiers shoot.
            Exeunt [marching. A peal of ordnance shot off].

362. *put on* instigated; *forced cause* by reason of   376. *put on* set to perform in office.
compulsion.   377. *passage* death.

Textual Commentary

The first edition of *Hamlet* was printed in quarto in 1603. It was published apparently without authorization—not surprisingly in view of the fact that it presents a pirated text of the play. This so-called "bad" quarto (Q1) is a reported text, put together from memory by a group of actors who had either seen the play performed, or who had themselves performed in it, on the London stage. Their purpose, presumably, was to furnish themselves with an acting version of the play to take on tour in the provinces. Most of their memories seem to have been drawn from the Shakespearean version of the tragedy, though it appears likely that memories of the pre-Shakespearean *Hamlet* have been incorporated at several points into the Q1 text. In it, Polonius is named Corambis (he is called Corambus in *Der Bestrafte Brudermord*). Reynaldo is Montano, and the nunnery scene occurs in Act II, immediately after Polonius/Corambis has made his suggestion to "loose" his daughter to Hamlet. In the Q1 version of the scene in Gertrude's chamber, the Queen explicitly denies having been a party to her husband's murder (thereby clearing up a point that is not clear in the more authoritative editions, and which Coleridge and other critics have wondered about), and she pledges herself to assist her son in his revenge. Q1 presents just the sort of garbled text that memorial reconstructions regularly do. The line of the action as we know it from the later editions is roughly preserved, though it is greatly simplified and vulgarized; and the Shakespearean language is thoroughly dissipated.

An authorized version of the play was duly published in the following year (the title pages of some copies of the second quarto bear the date 1604, others are dated 1605). All the evidence—especially that of the stage directions—suggests that this second quarto (Q2) was printed from Shakespeare's own manuscript. It is the fullest text of the play that survives (almost 3800 lines, as opposed to the 2220 type-lines of Q1), and the most authoritative, though its authority is somewhat diminished as a result of the many compositorial errors and omissions made in the process of printing, and also as a result of the fact that the bad first quarto was frequently consulted, for whatever reason, during the early stages of the printing of Q2, so that what should be, and in most respects is, the most authoritative text of the play has been contaminated at sundry points throughout the first act from the reported text of Q1.

A third quarto (Q3), printed from Q2, was published in 1611; and sometime between then and 1623 a fourth quarto (Q4, undated), printed from Q3, appeared. Neither Q3 nor Q4 has any independent textual authority.

The text of *Hamlet* that appeared in the folio collection (F) of Shakespeare's complete works in 1623 is generally supposed to have been printed from—or at least to have had behind it, if it were not directly printed from—the official theatrical promptbook. Thus it presumably represents the play as it had come to be acted by the King's Men some twenty years after its original production. It omits some 230 lines found in Q2, though it contains some 80 lines that are missing from Q2. There are numerous verbal differences between the two texts. Many of these are compositorial errors, occasioned when either the Q2 or the F workmen misread their manuscript. Examples are such variants as "cap" (F), "lap" (Q2), at II.ii.222; "loneliness" (F), "lowliness" (Q2), at III.i.46; "feature" (F), "stature" (Q2), at III.i.155; "so loud a wind" (F), "so loved Arm'd" (Q2), at IV.vii.22; "argal" (F), "or all" (Q2), at V.i.10, where in each case, F gives a correct reading for what is a literal misprint in Q2. But the folio has its share of compositional misreadings as well. The "time" (Q2), "tune" (F) variant at III.i.154 is an example of one that has long been received into editions of the play. The famous case of the "sallied" (Q2) vs. the "solid" (F) flesh that Hamlet wishes, at I.ii.129, would melt, is almost certainly another.[1]

Not all the instances where F displays a word or phrase different from the corresponding reading in Q2 are due, however, to compositorial misreadings. There is no decisive evidence for supposing that the folio text represents a Shakespearean revision of the play as it appears in Q2, though this is sometimes argued. And assuming that the folio text derives from the official promptbook, and thus reflects theatrical practices, there is good reason to suppose that, where F departs from Q2 and a compositor is not responsible, the F variants represent verbal changes that had come to be made in the text by the actors themselves, over the years during which the play was performed. The folio text of *Hamlet* exhibits, in fact, just the sort of changes that one might expect to take place in the language of a play that had been in an active theatrical repertory for two decades. By comparison with the text of Q2, the actors can be seen taking certain liberties with their lines. Verbal substitutions have been made, catch words and phrases are repeated, and most troublesome of all perhaps, as Professor Harold Jenkins has pointed out in an important article,[2] the actors have interpolated a number of "gag lines" into their parts, of which the "Oh Vengeance" that F (but not Q2) interjects midway through Hamlet's soliloquy at the close of the second act is the most egregious.

For all its typographical imperfections, the second quarto gives us a text of *Hamlet* that must be regarded as superior to that of the folio, not only because it is fuller, but because it is closer to a Shakespearean manuscript source. It is the basis of the present edition. The folio text has been regularly consulted, and readings from it have been received into the present edition to supply Q2 omissions of words and phrases, to correct Q2 misprints, and to emend other corruptions in the Q2 text. The folio is, of course, the authority for the longer passages omitted from Q2 (as, for instance, at II.ii.231–58; II.ii.315–35; V.ii.68–80). The precise extent of my use of the folio text,

1. For persuasive arguments that both Q2 readings here are the right ones, see G. W. Williams, "Hamlet's Reason, Jangled out of Time: III.i.166," *Notes and Queries* 205 (1960): 329–31; and F. T. Bowers, "Hamlet's 'Sullied' or 'Solid' Flesh. A Bibliographical Case-History," *Shakespeare Survey* 9 (1956): 44–47.

2. "Playhouse Interpolations in the Folio Text of *Hamlet*," *Studies in Bibliography* 13 (1960): 31–47.

and of all other editions of the play apart from Q2, is shown in the Textual Notes, where all substantive departures from the text of the second quarto are recorded. The Q2 spelling has been modernized for the present edition, and the punctuation has been silently emended where intelligibility has seemed to require it. I have sought, however, to retain wherever possible the relatively light Q2 system of pointing, which is often highly revealing, chiefly, one would like to suppose, because it reflects at a not too distant remove Shakespeare's own intentions. The stage directions of this edition are those of the second quarto. Editorial additions to them are enclosed in square brackets. Strong preterit verb endings are marked with an acute accent (´) in verse passages where the meter requires that they be stressed.

TEXTUAL NOTES

Emendations of the second quarto text received into the present edition are printed inside the square bracket with—to the right of the bracket—an abbreviated reference to the edition in which the emendation first appears. The rejected Q2 reading follows. *om.* means *omitted.* Editions are referred to by the following abbreviations:

Q1	Quarto, 1603
Q2	Quarto, 1604–5
Q3	Quarto, 1611
Q4	Quarto, Undated
Q5	Quarto, 1637
F	Folio, 1623
F2	Folio, 1632

The following later editions also cited in the notes, by name: Rowe (1709); Pope (1723–25); Theobald (1733); Hanmer (1744); Warburton (1747); Johnson (1765); Capell (1767–68); Malone (1790); Collier (1842–44); Keightley (1867); Furness (1877); New Cambridge (1934).

[I.i] 16. soldier] *F*; souldiers *Q2*. 44. harrows] *F*; horrowes *Q2*. 45. Question it] *F*; Speak to it *Q2*. 73. why] *F*; with *Q2*. 73. cast] *F*; cost *Q1–2*. 88. those] *F*; these *Q2*. 91. returned]*F*; returne *Q2*. 94. designed] *Pope*; desseigne *Q2*; designe *F*. 112. moth] *Q4*; moth *Q2*; *om. F*. 121. feared] *Collier*; feare *Q2*; *om. F*. 138. you] *Q1*, *F*; your *Q2*. 140. at] *F*; *om. Q2*.
[I.ii] S.D. Councillors] Counsaile: as *Q2*. 58. He]*Q1,3,F*; *om. Q2*. 67. Not so, my] *F*; Not so much my *Q2*. 77. coold *Q2*. 82. shapes] *Q3*; chapes *Q2*; shewes *F*. 96. a mind] *F*; or minde *Q2*. 132. self] *F*; seale *Q2*. 133. weary] *F*; wary *Q2*. 137. come to this] *F*; come thus *Q2*. 143. would] *Q1,F*; should *Q2*. 175. you to drink deep ere] *Q1,F*; you for to drink ere *Q2*. 178. see] *Q1,F*; *om. Q2*. 235. hundred] *Q1,F*; hundreth *Q2*. 254. Foul] *Q1,F*; fonde *Q2*.

[I.iii] 3. is] *F*; in *Q2*. 12. bulk] *F*; bulkes *Q2*. 18. For he * * * birth] *F*; *om. Q2*. 49. like] *F*; *om. Q2*. 74. Are]*Q1,F*; Or *Q2*. 75. be] *F*; boy *Q2*. 76. loan] *F*; loue *Q2*. 77. dulls th'] *F7*; dulleth *Q2*. 83. invites] *F*; inuests *Q2*. 109. Running] *Collier*; tendring *Q1*; Wrong *Q2*; Roaming *F*. 115. springes] *Q1,F*; springs *Q2*. 125. tether] *F*; tider *Q2*. 130. bawds] *Theobald*; bonds *Q2,F*. 131. beguile] *Q3,F*; beguide *Q2*.
[I.iv] 2 a] *F*; *om.*, *Q2*. 19. clepe]*Q5*;clip *Q2*; *om. F*. 27. the]*Pope*; their *Q2*; *om. F*. 36. evil] *Keightley*; eale *Q2*; *om. F*. 37. often doubt] *Collier*; of a doubt *Q2*; *om. F*.
[I.v] 20. fretful] *Q1,F*; fearefull *Q2*. 47. a] *F*; *om. Q2*. 55. lust] *Q1,F*; but *Q2*. 56. sate] *Q1,F*; sort *Q2*. 68. posset] *F*; possesse *Q2*. 95. stiffly] *F*; swiftly *Q2*. 116. bird] *F*; and *Q2*. 122. my lord] *Q1,F*; *om. Q2*.
[II.i] S.D. with his man] with his man or two

Q2. 28. no] F; *om. Q2.* 38. warrant] F; wit
Q2. 40. i' th'] F; with Q2. 62. takes] F; take
Q2. 104. passion] F; passions Q2.
[II.ii] 57. o'erhasty]F; hastie Q2. 90. since]F;
om. Q2. 97. he is] F; hee's Q2. 125. above]
F; about Q2. 136. winking] F; working Q2.
142. his] Q3,F; her Q2. 148. a] F; *om. Q2.*
150. 'tis] F; *om. Q2.* 206. sanity] F; sanctity
Q2. 207–8. suddenly * * * between him and]
F; *om. Q2.* 218. excellent] Q3,F; extent Q2.
221. over-happy] F; euer happy Q2. 222. cap]
F; lap Q2. 230. that] F; *om. Q2.* 231–58.
Let me question * * * dreadfully attended]
F; *om. Q2.* 288. What a piece] F; What peece
Q2. 303–4. the clown * * * sere] F, where
"tickle" reads "tickled"; *om. Q2.* 315–35.
How comes it * * * load too] F; *om. Q2.*
319. berattle] F2; be-rattled F. 325. most like]
Pope; like most F. 344. lest] F; let Q2. 344.
my] Q3,F; me Q2. 366–67. tragical-histor-
ical . . . pastoral] F; *om. Q2.* 390. By'r] F;
by Q2. 394. French falconers] Q1,F; friendly
Fankners Q2. 405. affectation] F; affection
Q2. 408. tale] F; talke Q2. 435. Then * * *
Ilium] F; *om. Q2.* 442. And like] F; Like
Q2. 456. fellies] Furness; follies Q2; fallies
F. 497. for a need] Q1,F; for need Q2. 498.
dozen or] Q1,F; dosen lines, or Q2. 510.
his] F; the Q2. 517. the cue for] F; that for
Q2. 540. father] Q3; *om. Q2,F.* 544. scul-
lion] F; stallyon Q2; scalion Q1. 556. devil
. . . devil] F; deale . . . deale Q2.
[III.i] 32. lawful espials] F; *om. Q2.* 33. We'll]
F; wee'le Q2. 46. loneliness] F; lowlines Q2.
55. Let's] F; *om. Q2.* 83. of us all] F; *om.*
Q2. 99. the] F; these Q2. 107. your honesty
should] F; you should Q2. 119. to] F; *om.*
Q2. 125. all] F; *om. Q2.* 141. lisp] F; list
Q2. 142. your ignorance] F; ignorance Q2.
148. expectancy] F; expectation Q2. 153.
that] F; what Q2. 155. feature] F; stature Q2.
184. unwatched] F; unmatcht Q2.
[III.ii] 8. tatters] F; totters Q2. 19. own feature]
F; feature Q2. 23. the which] F; which Q2.
25. praise] F; praysd Q2. 80. detecting] F;
detected Q2. 102–3. I mean * * * lord] F;
om. Q2. 123. this is miching mallecho] F;
this munching *Mallico* Q2. 125. counsel] F;
om. Q2. 138. orbed ground] F; orb'd the
ground Q2. 146. your] F; our Q2. 148–49.
must. / For women's] F; must. / For women
feare too much, euen as they loue, / And
womens Q2. 150. In neither aught] F; Eyther
none, in neither ought Q2. 151. love] F; Lord
Q2. 181. joys] F; joy Q2. 201. An] *Theobald*; And Q2; *om.* F. 205. once a widow]
F; once I be a widdow Q2. 205. be wife]
Q4,F; be a wife Q2. 234. Confederate] Q1,F:
Considerat Q2. 236. infected] Q1,F; inuected
Q2. 243. What * * * fire] Q1,F; *om. Q2.*
253. two] F; *om. Q2.* 281. start] F; stare Q2.
290. my] F; *om. Q2.* 327. thumb] F; the
vmber Q2. 334. the top of] F; *om. Q2.* 337–
38, can fret me] F; fret me not Q2. 349–50.
Pol. I will say so. / *Ham.* 'By and by' is easily
said. Leave me, friends.] F; *Ham.* * * *

/ Leaue me friends. / I will, say so. By and
by is easily said, Q2. 352. breathes] F; breakes
Q2. 354. bitter business as the day] F; business as the bitter day Q2. 359. daggers] F;
dagger Q2.
[III.iii] 17. It is] F; or it is Q2. 19. huge] F;
hough Q2. 22. ruin] F; raine Q2. 23. with]
F; *om. Q2.* 50. pardoned] F; pardon Q2.
58. shove] F; showe Q2. 73. pat] F; but Q2.
79. hire and salary] F; base and silly Q2.
[III.iv] 5. warrant] F; wait Q2. 19. inmost] F;
most Q2. 53. That roars * * * index] F; line
assigned to Hamlet in Q2. 60. a heaven-
kissing] F; a heaue, a kissing Q2. 89. pan-
ders] F; pardons Q2. 90. eyes into my very
soul] F; very eyes into my soule Q2. 91.
grained] F; greeued Q2. 92. will not leave
their tinct] F; will leaue there their tinct Q2.
98. tithe] F; kyth Q2. 147. I] F; *om. Q2.*
162. live]F; leaue Q2. 169. Refrain to-night]
F; to refraine night Q2. 173. curb] *Malone*;
om. Q2,F. 219. a foolish] F; a most foolish
Q2.
[IV.i] 40. so * * * slander] *Capell*; *om. Q2,F.*
[IV,ii] 4. Compounded] Q3,F; Compound Q2.
26. Hide * * * after] F; *om. Q2.*
[IV.iii] 40. With * * * quickness] F; *om. Q2.*
64. were ne'er begun] F; will nere begin Q2.
[IV.v] 9. aim] F; yawn Q2. 16. *Queen.* Let her
come in.]F; speech assigned to Horatio in
Q2. 38. grave] F; ground Q2. 80. their] F;
om. Q2. 87. his] F; this Q2. 95. are] Q3,F;
is Q2. 104. They] F; The Q2. 140. swoop-
stake] Q1; soopstake Q2,F. 150. Let her come
in] F; assigned to Laertes in Q2. 155. Till]
F; Tell Q2. 158. an old] F; a poor Q2. 159–
61. Nature * * * it loves] F; *om. Q2.* 163.
Hey * * * hey nonny] F; *om. Q2.* 177. O,
you must] F; you may Q2. 181. affliction]
F; afflictions Q2. 189. All] F; *om. Q2.* 193.
I pray God] F; *om. Q2.* 194. see] F; *om. Q2.*
[IV.vi] 18. good] F; *om. Q2.* 21. bore] F; bord
Q2. 25. He] F; So Q2. 26. give] F; *om. Q2.*
[IV.vii] 6. proceeded] F; proceede Q2. 14,
conjunctive] F; concliue Q2. 22. so loud a
wind] F; so loued Arm'd Q2. 24. had] F;
have Q2. 44. and more strange] F; *om. Q2.*
54. shall] F; *om. Q2.* 60. As checking] F; As
the King Q2. 86. my] F; me Q2. 113. wick]
Rowe; weeke Q2. 132. on] F; ore Q2. 138.
that] F; *om. Q2.* 165. hoar] F; horry Q2.
169. cold] F; cull-cold Q2.
[V.i] 8. "se offendendo"] F; so offended Q2.
10. argal] F; or all Q2. 29–31. *Other.* Why,
he had none. / *Clown.* What, * * * without
arms?] F; *om. Q2.* 37. frame] F; *om. Q2.*
48.1. *afar off*] F; *om. Q2.* 52. stoup] F; soope
Q2. 57. that] F; *om. Q2.* 78. mazzard] F;
massene Q2. 92–93. Is this the fine of his
fines, and the recovery of his recoveries] F;
om. Q2. 94. Will his vouchers] F; will
vouchers Q2. 94–95. double ones too] F;
doubles Q2. 104. O] F; or Q2. 122 all] F;
om. Q2. 143; now-a-days] F; *om. Q2.* 150.
three and twenty years] F; 23 years Q2. 166.
chamber] F; table Q2. 186. winter's] F; waters

Q2. 201. Shards] *F; om. Q2*. 217. times tre-
ble] *F;* times double *Q2*. 231. and] *F; om.
Q2*. 261. thus] *F;* this *Q2*. 270. shortly] *F;*
thereby *Q2*.
[V.ii] 5. Methought]*F;* my thought *Q2*. 9. pall]
F; fall *Q2*. 17. unseal] *F;* unfold *Q2*. 43.
as's] *F* (Assis); as sir *Q2*. 57. Why, man * * *
employment] *F; om. Q2*. 68–80. To quit
* * * comes here] *F; om. Q2*. 73. interim
is] *Hanmer;* interim's *F*. 78. court] *Rowe;*
count *F; om. Q2*. 82. humbly] *F;* humble
Q2.91. Put] *F; om. Q2*. 96. sultry] *Q3,F;*
sully *Q2*. 96. for] *F;* or *Q2*. 131. his] *Q5;*
this *Q2*. 138. hangers] *F;* hanger *Q2*. 146.
might be] *Q3,F;* be might *Q2*. 149.

impawned] *New Cambridge; om. Q2;*
impon'd *F*. 149. as] *F; om Q2*. 164 He] *F;
om. Q2*. 167. comply]*F;* so *Q2*. 168. bevy]
F; breede *Q2*. 170. yesty] *F;* histy *Q2*. 171.
fanned] *Warburton;* prophane *Q2;* fond *F*.
171. winnowed] *F;* trennowed *Q2*. 195. be
now, 'tis] *F;* be, tis *Q2*. 214. Sir, in this
audience] *F; om. Q2*. 224. keep] *F; om. Q2*.
224. till] *F;* all *Q2*. 237. bettered] *F;* better
Q2. 246. union] *F;* Onixe *Q2*. 276. afeard]
F; sure *Q2*. 292. Hamlet, thou] *F;*thou *Q2*.
295. thy] *F;* my *Q2*. 304. murd'rous] *F; om.
Q2*. 305. thy union] *F;* the Onixe *Q2*. 358.
th' yet] *Q3, F;* yet *Q2*. 362. forced] *F;* for no
Q2. 371. on] *F;* no *Q2*.